CONRAD FERDINAND MEYER

LONDON : HUMPHREY MILFORD

OXFORD UNIVERSITY PRESS

CONRAD FERDINAND MEYER
The Style and the Man

BY ARTHUR BURKHARD

1932

Cambridge, Massachusetts

HARVARD UNIVERSITY PRESS

PT
2432
.Z9
B8

"... ich bin kein ausgeklügelt Buch,
Ich bin ein Mensch mit seinem Widerspruch..."

PREFACE

THE purpose and procedure of this attempt to develop the personality of Conrad Ferdinand Meyer from a study of the style of his works have been presented in the opening chapter, the first part of which sets forth the aim, method, and manner of presentation of this treatise. The second part of the first chapter completes the introduction by portraying the struggle for expression experienced by Meyer, which resulted in the employment in his poetry and prose of those characteristic artistic devices upon which this investigation of the style and the man are based. These prefatory remarks need add nothing, therefore, by way of exposition of purpose, explanation of method, or apology for the manner of treatment: "Der Worte sind genug gewechselt,/Lasst mich auch endlich Taten seh'n."

There remains for the preface, accordingly, only the duty of acknowledging in print indebtedness which can be more simply and sincerely discharged by word of mouth: "Wie nimmt ein leidenschaftlich Stammeln/Geschrieben sich so seltsam aus!" Comforted by the compact sentiment of Moscherosch, "Dank sind dankbare Gedanken," I here purposely abstain from compiling an unwieldy list of the various persons in America, Germany, Switzerland, and

France with whom it has been my privilege to discuss and study problems connected with Conrad Ferdinand Meyer. I cannot refrain from recalling, however, the kindness of Frau Camilla Meyer, the daughter of the poet, who accorded me permission to visit his home in Kilchberg and inspect his library; of Adolf Frey, Meyer's friend and first biographer, who allowed me to consult him during the illness which soon thereafter resulted in his death; of Eduard Korrodi, pioneer in appraising Meyer's style, who received me during a busy morning in the editorial rooms of the *Neue Zürcher Zeitung*; of Max Rychner, friend and fellow-student, who sat beside me in the Meyer-Seminar of Emil Ermatinger twelve years ago and who has since become a Meyer editor and author in his own right; and finally of Robert d'Harcourt, acutest of Meyer critics, whose spirited conversations concerning Conrad Ferdinand Meyer carried on in his summer home near Rheims and in his winter apartment in Paris, have been a lasting stimulus and source of inspiration to me.

Among my more immediate colleagues, I owe gratitude to Professors H. C. Bierwirth and J. A. Walz of Harvard University, both of whom read my manuscript with care and recommended several changes which I was glad to incorporate in the text and in the notes. Likewise to my friend and former colleague, Dr. H. H. Stevens, with whom I have discussed stylistic matters for more than fifteen years and who has allowed me during this time to profit from his intimate acquaintance with the problems pertaining to Meyer's style. I am further indebted for help in reading the proof to two of my former students who are at present instructors in German at Harvard, Messrs. Alan Holske and R. H. Phelps: "I can no other answer make but thanks,/And thanks and ever thanks; and oft good turns/Are shuffled off with such uncurrent pay."

Harvard University has been generous in its assistance by awarding me several years ago a Frederick Sheldon Travelling Fellowship which enabled me to continue my studies in Switzerland, and by paying a part of the expenses of publication of this volume from the fund for the support of the humanities provided by the General Education Board.

ARTHUR BURKHARD

CAMBRIDGE, MASSACHUSETTS
February, 1932

CONTENTS

I. INTRODUCTION 3
    1. Aim, Method, Manner of Presentation
    2. The Struggle for Expression

II. THE GRAND STYLE AND MANNER 28

III. CONCRETE FORMS AND MOVING FIGURES . . . 66

IV. CONCLUSION 122
    1. The Principle of Polarity
    2. The Attainment of Form

NOTES 161

BIBLIOGRAPHY 219

CONRAD FERDINAND MEYER

I

INTRODUCTION

I. AIM, METHOD, MANNER OF PRESENTATION

Bleibt mir vom Leib mit nichtigen Zahlen.

ALTHOUGH we commonly accept in theory the belief that the style is the man, we have made comparatively few practical applications of this principle in our critical contributions which concern themselves with literary productions. Scholarly research in our country has customarily appeared content to restrict itself to matters of biographical detail in the lives of authors, or to studies of the sources and influences of their works. We realize, apparently, that in establishing the contribution made by artistic tradition or by the experience of the poet to a work of the creative imagination, we are not treating the essential elements which give it life and lasting influence: "Nescis unde veniat, aut quo vadat: sic est omnis qui natus est ex spiritu."[1] We are altogether ready to agree with Goethe: "Die Frage: Woher hat's der Dichter? geht auch nur aufs Was; vom Wie erfährt dabei niemand etwas,"[2] yet we continue to concern ourselves in our critical endeavors with the mere externals of literary works. Rarely do our professional journals print investigations of the style of a finished

literary product; almost never appear, there or elsewhere, articles that seek to evolve the personality of a
poet from his writings or endeavor to portray his
character as revealed in the style of his collected
works. Yet such examination would seem to be a
more important sphere for our activities, much more
in keeping with the purpose of our profession, more in
accord, finally, with the tenet attributed to Buffon,
"Le style, c'est l'homme même."

Schopenhauer, in fact, went so far as to write to
Goethe, "Was ich denke, was ich schreibe, das hat für
mich Werth und ist mir wichtig: was ich persönlich
erfahre und was sich mit mir zuträgt, ist mir Neben-
sache, ja ist mein Spott."[1] Conrad Ferdinand Meyer,
more conservative in temperament, much more reserved in statements about his own life, for reasons
which we shall later discover, merely remarked to his
sister Betsy, "Mein Lebenslauf ist im Grunde un-
glaublich merkwürdig. Wie werden sie einst daran
herumrätseln,"[2] leaving it for her to make clear that
the riddle of his remarkable life could be solved only
after a consideration of his works: "Die tiefliegenden
Quellen seines Lebens blieben zugedeckt. . . . Wer
des Dichters innerstes Wesen kennen will, findet es
allein in seinen Werken."[3] From these works, however, their author was careful to remove almost all
direct references to his surroundings, preferring the
form of the historical romance to treatments of contemporary material because such subject matter, he

says, serves as a mask to conceal his own experiences and sentiments. To his friend Felix Bovet he wrote, "Je me sers de la forme de la nouvelle historique purement et simplement pour y loger mes expériences et mes sentiments personnels, la préférant au Zeitroman, parce qu'elle me masque mieux et qu'elle distance davantage le lecteur. Ainsi, sous une forme très objective et éminemment artistique, je suis au dedans tout individuel et subjectif. Dans tous les personnages du Pescara, même dans ce vilain Morone, il y a du C. F. M."[1]

It is extremely difficult, however, to discover traits of Meyer in Morone or, for that matter, in most of his characters. Just as the settings of his stories are far removed from him in time and place, so many of his characters seem to resemble his opposite much more than his own image, forming a curious contrast to the picture we get of him in his letters or contemporary accounts of his life. If the setting, subject matter, and characters of these works do not readily reveal the personality of their author, there still remains the style, to which Meyer calls attention as a key to his own character. To Joseph Victor Widman he writes, "Mein starkes Stylisiren — wie es G. Keller zwischen Tadel und Lob nannte und *meine besonders künstlich zubereiteten Wirkungen* müssen mir *im Blute stecken.* Freilich, wer kennt sich selbst!"[2]

In order to know Meyer, let us examine carefully, therefore, the "strongly pronounced stylizing" and

"the artificially prepared effects" which Keller discovered in his work and which Meyer feels must be
"in his blood." In penetrating the secret of his style,
we may also solve the riddle of his "problematical
nature" and through an examination of his art arrive
at an understanding of his complex and puzzling personality, which has not always been correctly ap-
praised.

To help me realize this aim, I have employed the
following method. In examining the verse and prose
of Meyer in the final revised version of what, for the
present, seems to remain the definitive edition,[1] I have
tried to penetrate through his words on the printed
page to the essential idea from which his sentence was
developed. Asking and seeking to answer the question, What did he mean by this? I have sought to
strip his sentences of all external adornments, leaving
only the thought exposed to view in its original naked-
ness, before it was clothed in its final form in the lines
of the stories or poems. Then, reversing the process, I
have sought to follow the life history of his thought
from the original germ to the final form of expression,
asking and seeking to answer the question, How did
he come to say it in this particular way?

As in translation one tries to look through the
words to the meaning underlying them, going below
the surface of the writer's mind to get the germ of his
thought before returning to the surface prepared to
put his meaning into another tongue, so in my exami-

nation of Meyer's works I have endeavored to reduce his poems and prose stories, line for line and word for word, to the barest essentials, in an attempt to discover the stylistic reason for their present formulation. Although it is exceedingly difficult to trace the path from thought to speech, to follow the life history of a thought from its original conception in another man's mind to its birth in utterance, it is comparatively simple to separate, in a general way, a writer's thought from his words, to discriminate between the intellectual and emotional, between the expressive elements of his art and the decorative, and to make a close and detailed study of the motives which have determined the particular forms of expression which he employs. This I have attempted to do in my examination of the poetry and prose of Conrad Ferdinand Meyer.[1]

The manner of presenting the material which this method yields had to be carefully considered in order to make possible the realization of my aim of interpreting correctly Meyer's personality on the basis of his style. To enumerate completely the almost endless lists of words and phrases which are the first result of such a critical analysis, even if they are properly grouped under various appropriate headings, would have resulted in a work of reference rather than a readable book. The practice of making an arbitrary choice, on the other hand, among the stylistic devices commonly employed by Meyer without some indication of the frequency of their occurrence, allows so much room for personal prejudice that two of my predecessors, indulging in this practice, have arrived at results almost diametrically opposed.[1] A third and more recent critic of Meyer's poetry and personality, scorning controversy with either of his predecessors, with one of whom he plainly disagrees, tries to rise superior to both in seeking out the peculiarities of Meyer's style, which he praises as perfection with more sympathetic than critical judgment.[2] To avoid the dangers of such capricious pronouncements, I have kept count of the occurrence of the common stylistic devices employed in Meyer's poetry and prose, and have incorporated directly in the text many of my examples to serve as proof that sometimes Meyer's manner becomes mere mannerism. In order to keep my text reasonably free from encumbering enumerations, however, and to preserve at least a fairly readable form, I have relegated the large bulk of the merely statistical material, whenever possible, to the notes, to which only those need turn who care to be assured of the origin or convinced of the accuracy of my statements. This procedure brings with it an unfortunate gain in volume and a necessary loss in lightness of touch, but also, it is hoped, the compensation of a closer approach to the truth.

The material which such a stylistic analysis yields has been assembled under two general headings. The first, entitled "The Grand Style and Manner," treats the nobility of expression characteristic of Meyer's style in explanation of his statement to his publisher Hermann Haessel, "Grosser Styl, Grosse Kunst, all mein Denken und Träumen liegt darin."[1] The second, entitled "Concrete Forms and Moving Figures," takes up in turn the qualities of precision and plasticity manifest in Meyer's verse and prose, in elaboration of his remark to his friend Hermann Friedrichs, "Plastisch greifbare Gestalten hervorzuzaubern und sie handelnd auftreten zu lassen, das ist eine Kunst, die nur verschwindend Wenigen gegeben ist."[2] These two main parts of the specialized analysis of Meyer's style are followed by a general conclusion which treats first, "The Principle of Polarity" in Meyer's life and work, and second, an appraisal of Meyer's accomplishment and of his place in the literature of Germany under the title "The Attainment of Form."

This Introduction, finally, which has heretofore merely set forth the "Aim, Method, and Manner of Presentation" of the material concerning the style of Conrad Ferdinand Meyer, is continued in a second section entitled "The Struggle for Expression," which reviews some of the more important statements made by Meyer in regard to his method of work and his attitude toward art, so that in the treatment of his style which follows we may see illustrated the principles which he formulates and which are eminently characteristic of him and his literary production.

2. THE STRUGGLE FOR EXPRESSION

Genug ist nicht genug!

To the immature architect entrusted with drawing plans for the cathedral in Conrad Ferdinand Meyer's poem *Das Münster*[1] there appears a saint with uplifted finger to pronounce the warning,

> Tändle nicht!
> Das Amt, das dir zu Lehen fiel,
> Das ist ein Werk und ist kein Spiel![2]

Perhaps in the struggles of his own early years, Meyer had heard and given heed to a similar warning; certainly, as he became mature, he grew impatient with playful trifling, ever more earnest and careful in his attitude toward his own life work. Rarely has an artist labored more with his art. His first biographer, Frey, comparing him apparently to an architect, testifies to his ethical energy and victory over self: "einen Bau, den er mühsam errichtet, bis auf den letzten Stein niederzureissen und von neuem aufzuführen."[3] His sister reports that his artistic conscience was never satisfied before he had undertaken a second and a third revision of a former unsatisfactory poem. If these proved fruitless he broke the verses apart and tried to recast them anew: "Ich habe den Stoff noch einmal in den Schmelztiegel geworfen. Er muss weiter glühen. Heute lässt er sich nicht schmieden."[4] This comparison of himself to a smith operating with molten metal he continues when he speaks of his works, "die auf der Esse liegen, und um welche noch die Flamme der Phantasie züngelt."[1] He changes the figure to compare himself to a sculptor when he writes to Rahn, "Ich stehe, wie Michel Angelo sagte, vor dem Stein und sage mir stündlich: Courage, es steckt darin, es handelt sich nur darum, es herauszukriegen."[2] He feels like a wrestler when he confides to a friend that he has found "einen herr-lichen Stoff... mit dem ich aber mühsam ringen muss, wenn ich ihm seinen Werth geben will"[3] — like the biblical wrestler, in fact, when he often repeats to Frey, "Ich halte es mit meinen Stoffen, wie Jakob mit dem Engel: ich ringe mit dir und lasse dich nicht, du segnest mich denn!", when he reassures him on hear-ing of his difficulties with rebellious literary problems, "O, wenn Sie wüssten, wie ich mit meinen Stoffen kämpfe!"[4]

For Meyer artistic production was a struggle, which became even more difficult through the exacting de-mands he made upon himself. His volume of verse opens with a poem whose first line, thereafter four times repeated, reads "Genug ist nicht genug!" only to close with a still more exacting last line, "Genug kann nie und nimmermehr genügen!"[5] When the muse in response to his imploring for an "Angebinde" places on his table "einer Ampel zarte Form," his first reaction is the query, "Was meinst du, Muse? Rätst du/Nächtlich auszufeilen meine Verse?"[6] Not slow to act on such a suggestion, he is tireless in the revisions of his poetry and prose, even after his works are already in print. His first long poem *Huttens letzte Tage* underwent changes for each one of the ten different editions;[1] of the second long poem, *Engelberg*, no less than seven versions are extant;[2] the poem *Zur neuen Auflage* in his collection of *Gedichte* commences with the line, "Mit dem Stifte les' ich diese Dinge."[3] From the original version printed in the *Deutsche Rundschau* to the first edition in book form, *Plautus im Nonnenkloster* shows fifty changes, *Die Richterin* about one hundred and ten, and *Die Hochzeit des Mönchs* as many as seven hundred and fifty.[4] These numbers are, of course, small, compared to the changes made before the manuscript went to press, and dwindle to insignificance when we consider the variants which teemed in Meyer's brain, so many of them that he confesses to Frey his inability to remember how many metamorphoses *Die Richterin* had undergone.[5]

Such revision was for him a labor of love. To his publisher he writes, "Schlagen Sie sich doch aus dem Kopfe, dass ich mich mit den Aenderungen *quäle*, im Gegentheil, es ist für mich ein Genuss, immer wieder den vollendeteren Ausdruck zu suchen."[6] This delight in seeking ever the more perfect expression finally degenerates into a fault. He lets himself become so disturbed by a single word that after observing in one letter "dass mir das 'und wurde

Purpur' auch nicht gefällt. Besser wäre: und wurde Flamme,"[1] he sends another message later the same day merely to indicate the final form for an ultimate revision, "Nein, lieber Freund, pg. 244 muss es weder Purpur, noch Flamme heissen, sondern Glut — 'und wurde Glut'."[2] Toward the close of his career, his careful concern with having the words appear perfect in print becomes almost neurotic in its persistence. For his last story he importunes his publisher in a veritable storm of letters, postscripts, and post-cards, "Drucken Sie ja genau!",[3] "Ja genau nach der Rundschau drucken!",[4] "Es darf kein Fehlerchen stehen bleiben!",[5] "Wir wollen eine ganz makellose Angela haben!";[6] until finally the editor of his correspondence refuses to reprint more of these demands, contenting himself with the footnote, "Fast jeden Tag schrieb C. F. Meyer damals eine oder zwei Karten an Haessel, immer mit der dringenden Bitte um möglichst sorgfältige Korrektur."[7] Little wonder that a modern critical aphorist phrases this failing as a fault, finding that "er litt an der Krankheit der Vollendung."[8]

While his countryman and contemporary Keller, with whom comparison seems inevitable,[9] appears able to compose with small effort, quite naturally, almost carelessly, Meyer was able to produce only by painstaking labor, after endless revisions. Keller's style seems the gift of divine genius, Meyer's the result of arduous endeavor and heroic struggle, as if he

felt, like his earlier compatriot Haller, that "leichte
Arbeit ist auch in der Poesie schlecht."[1] Meyer possessed genius only in the sense of Goethe's definition
of genius as industry, "Genie und Fleiss"; only by
hard labor and application did he develop his masterpieces. His talent was not a spontaneous but a reflective one; he was not a naïve poet, but a highly conscious artist; his literary productions are the result of
much meditation, they are all carefully planned, ar-
tistically constructed, almost fastidiously composed,
never the result of a spontaneous overflow of emotion. "Seine Schöpfungen waren nicht die raschen
Kinder glücklicher, behaglicher Stunden," his friend
and first biographer, Frey, reports: "Es war auch be-
zeichnend, dass er selbst bei heiterster Laune, in der
angeregtesten Stunde niemals auch nur eine Zeile im-
provisierte oder aus dem Stegreif zum besten gab."[2]
He reminds one in every respect of those superior
people whom Goethe described to Eckermann: "Es
giebt vortreffliche Menschen, die nichts aus dem
Stegreife, nichts obenhin zu tun vermögen, sondern
deren Natur es verlangt, ihre jedesmaligen Gegenstände mit Ruhe zu durchdringen. Solche Talente
machen uns oft ungeduldig, indem man selten von
ihnen erlangt, was man augenblicklich wünscht;
allein auf diesem Wege, wird das Höchste geleistet."[3]
Meyer wanted to reach the heights, to rise above
the trivialities of everyday life in art, to worship at
the shrine of art as in a temple. Frequently Frey

heard him confess, "Die Kunst hebt uns wie nichts anderes über die Trivialitäten dieses Daseins hinweg. Ehe sich Machiavell zum Schreiben niedersetzte, zog er sein Feierkleid an. Ein verwandtes Gefühl überkommt mich, wenn ich mich an die Arbeit begebe. Mir ist, ich betrete die Schwelle eines Tempels."[1] The sacred flame of art he cherished in his bosom:

> Und ich hüte sie mit heil'ger Scheue,
> Dass sie brenne rein und ungekränkt.[2]

The goal of his struggle with art, of his striving for expression, was the grand style and manner, in which he confesses his thinking and dreaming was concentrated: "*Grosser* Styl, *Grosse* Kunst — all mein Denken und Träumen liegt darin."[3] In his analysis of *Der Heilige* for Hermann Lingg, he underscores the "*Grosse* Scenen," calls attention to the "*Grosser* Stil."[4] He is like his hero Pescara, "der das *Grosse* liebt";[5] like his Cangrande, "der von *grosser* Gesinnung war";[6] like the heroine of *Die Richterin*, "die *grosse* Sünderin," who remarks, "Wulfrin, du hast recht gesagt, was ich thue, thue ich *gross*." [7] He has no comprehension for the unintelligent *nil admirari* of the courtiers of the same story assembled on the square before the capitol in Rome, "sich über nichts verwundern wollend, was ihnen die ewige Stadt *Grosses* und Ehrwürdiges vor das Auge stellte."[8] When he is borne "nach Rom, der ew'gen Stadt,"[9] he finds in the eternal city and takes back home with him the sense of grandeur which they overlook, and which remains his for life:

> Den Ernst des Lebens nehm' ich mit mir fort;
> Den *Sinn des Grossen* raubt mir keiner mehr;
> Ich nehme der Gedanken reichen Hort
> Nun über Land und Meer.[1]

Of the impressions of his trip to Rome and of his discovery there of Michel Angelo, his sister reports, "Nun kam er nach Rom and sah die Sistina Michel Angelos. Diese Kunst traf ihn wie ein Lichtblitz. Buonarotti erschien ihm in seinen Schöpfungen als der *grösste* Poet. Hier stand vor seinem Blicke, was er immer gesucht hatte: gewaltige Verkörperung *grosser* Gedanken."[2] The glorious creations of Renaissance artists in Rome, and elsewhere in Italy, represented his artistic ideals and opened up large perspectives for him. In Titian he finds "Schönheit und *grosse* Geberde," and he sums up his Italian experience to a friend, "Es fiel mir wie Schuppen von den Augen."[3]

To Gottfried Keller he afterward declared, "Ich muss mit der *grossen* Historie fahren."[4] To Kögel he comments on his preference for the great personalities of the Renaissance who felt free to reveal themselves with all their faults: "Ich nehme gern Helden, die im irdischen Leben hoch stehen, damit sie Fallhöhe haben für ihren Sturz. Unter einem General tu ich's nicht gern mehr."[5] Earlier he had written to his publisher, "Unter einem Kaiser und Kanzler thue ich es einmal nicht mehr. . . ."[1] He recruits his heroes, accordingly, from generals, chancellors, kings, emperors, and popes, who occupy high stations in life and are perched on the highest summits of history, somewhat resembling in their large outlines the world apart, the race of giants, in Meyer's phrase, which Michel Angelo created in his anatomical studies and in stone.[2] Achilles, Alexander, Becket, Bismarck, Caesar, Caesar Borgia, Camoëns, Cellini, Cromwell, Dante, Dionysos, Frederick II, Huss, Luther, Michel Angelo, Milton, Napoleon, Petrarch, Raphael, Schiller, Socrates, Titian, Vercingetorix [3] — these are the august associates of Meyer and the great characters of his verse and prose. These characters, and others like them in Meyer's works, are men whom young Goethe would have termed "dämonisch," whom young Schiller, recalling Rousseau's praise of the heroes in Plutarch's *Lives*, characterizes as "keine halbgrossen Menschen . . . sondern grosse Tugendhafte und erhabene Verbrecher."[4] They all have claim to greatness, whether in virtue or vice, and some among them might well exclaim with Meyer's Italian friend Baron Ricasoli, "N'importe que je sois malheureux, pourvu que je sois grand."[5]

This desire and respect for grandeur accounts in part for Meyer's love of the lofty Alps of his native land that seemed to satisfy, his sister explains, his "Bedürfnis nach *Grösse*."[6] When he builds a house for himself he is, as a matter of fact, careful to have "kein

Zimmer weniger als zwölf Fuss hoch,"[1] resembling in
this respect his hero Wulfrin, who has "die Gewohn-
heit breiter Ebenen und *grosser* Räume."[2] Finding
Switzerland too small[3] and the dream of a specifically
Swiss literature "ein baarer Unsinn,"[4] he feels convinced "dass Zusammenhang und Anschluss an das
grosse deutsche Leben für uns Schweizer etwas
Selbstverständliches und Notwendiges ist," as they
already belong to "einer *grossen* nationalen Kultur."[5]
To Rodenberg he writes that his love for Germany
was in the last analysis "die Sehnsucht und das Bedürfnis, einem *grossen* Ganzen anzugehören."[6] To
Haessel he cries, "Lassen Sie sich doch in Teufels
Namen von Bismarck zu einer *grossen* und herrschen-
den Nation machen!",[7] feeling affection for Germany
because it was large and for Bismarck because he had
made it so and had become thereby the greatest personality of his times.[8]

It was not merely "Die Wollust, einen grossen
Mann zu sehen," as Goethe's Bruder Martin remarks,
that enticed Meyer to the historical past.[9] He
shunned the present and turned to treat the past in
his stories because he found contemporary times too
near, too raw, too brutal, too revelatory. Twice in
letters to Louise von François he explained this preference for the historical: "Es ist seltsam, mit meinem
(ohne Selbstlob) geübten Auge komme ich oft in Versuchung Gegenwart zu schildern: aber dann trete ich
plötzlich davor zurück. Es ist mir zu roh und zu

nah...";[1] "Am liebsten vertiefe ich mich in vergangene Zeiten, deren Irrtümer ich leise ironisiere,
und die mir erlauben, das Ewig-menschliche künstlerischer zu behandeln, als die brutale Aktualität zeitgenössischer Stoffe mir nicht gestatten würde."[2] We
remember, furthermore, that Meyer explained his
preference for the historical *Novelle* on the ground
that it removes the reader farther and helps to conceal
his own person.[3]

For these reasons among others, Meyer forsakes the
ordinary world of everyday commonplace for the historical, the heroic, the sublime, introducing into the
historical *Novelle*, as he proudly asserted, "den Stil
der *grossen* Tragödie."[4] In his historical romances
he never loses himself in antiquarian detail. In writing to his scholarly adviser Rahn for historical infor-
mation for the background of his stories, he is careful
to append to his request the injunction, "Natürlich
kein antiquarisches Detail, sondern nur ein paar
grosse, eigenthümliche Züge lokaler Wahrheit."[5]
For with the "Sinn des *Grossen*" is coupled "der Sinn
für das Erhabene."[6] Like his hero Dante, who smiles
only once during the course of the narrative,[7] Meyer
forsakes serious tragedy once only in his entire series
of stories, and then merely to hold to his promised
word. "Sie schlagen den 'Schuss' entschieden zu
hoch an," he writes to Wille, "ohne die Nötigung
des gegebenen Wortes wäre die Posse ungeschrieben
geblieben," adding as a general comment, "Mir in-

dividuell hinterlässt das Komische immer einen bittern Geschmack, während das Tragische mich erhebt und beseligt."[1] Gottfried Keller had already discovered Meyer's delight in tragedy. "Allein Meyer hat eine Schwäche für solche einzelne Brutalitäten und Totschläge," he writes to Storm in regard to *Jürg Jenatsch*, which closes, Storm finds, with a brutal "Fleischhauertat."[2]

Forsaking the present, the comic, the commonplace, to portray the historical past, the tragic, the sublime, the same Meyer who does not shrink from portraying such bloodshed and gruesome tragedy as the blow of an axe inflicts in *Jürg Jenatsch* remains at other times very restrained. The description of Wulfrin's treatment of his sister, for instance, is most summary and reserved;[3] other unseemly actions are only mentioned and then left to the imagination: "Welcher Mund den andern suchte, weiss ich nicht";[4] "Was sie sah, bleibt ungewiss . . . dass [aber] das schwere Gewölbe eine hässliche Scene verbarg — solches lese ich in dem verzerrten und entsetzten Gesichte der Lauscherin."[5] Unrefined or unaristocratic words are forgotten or inhibited or excused: "Das Uebrige vergass ich, aber ich weiss Eines: alle Jünglinge . . . wendeten Ohr und Auge ab";[6] "Sie hielt inne, um das reine Ohr Stemmas nicht zu beleidigen";[7] "einen Viehkerl, wenn ich das Wort vor den Ohren der Majestät aussprechen darf."[8] Like his character Louis XIV, Meyer seems to have fol-

lowed the rule, "Niemals, auch nicht erzählungsweise, ein gemeines oder beschimpfendes, kurz ein
unkönigliches Wort in den Mund zu nehmen."[1] We
may say of Meyer what he wrote of Astorre, "Das
Gemeine konnte den Mönch nicht berühren."[2] His
characters, moving in circles where discretion is common, remain, like him, aristocratic and reserved,[3] resembling his Astorre: "Der Druck der auf ihn ge-
richteten Aufmerksamkeit und die so zu sagen in der
Luft fühlbaren Formen und Forderungen der Gesellschaft liessen ihn empfinden, dass er nicht die
Wirklichkeit der Dinge sagen dürfe, energisch und
mitunter hässlich wie sie ist, sondern ihr eine ge-
milderte und gefällige Gestalt geben müsse. So hielt
er sich unwillkürlich in der Mitte zwischen Wahrheit
und schönem Sein und redete untadelig."[4] Like his
Ludwig Ariost, Meyer displays delicacy of feeling;
careful not to press rudely on the feelings of others,
or to pry into their private thoughts, "[Er] hütete
sich, auf ein Gefühl, das er an sich selbst nicht kannte
... unzart zu drücken ... weil er jedes fremde Ein-
greifen in einen Seelenvorgang als Gewaltthat ver-
abscheute."[5]

For Meyer felt that utilizing the feeling or physiog-
nomy of others as material for his stories was nothing
less than "Schamlosigkeit."[6] He lets a character cry,
"Welche Schamlosigkeit, sein Gewissen zu enthül-
len";[7] he selects "la nouvelle historique" in which to
lodge his personal feeling, as we have seen, "parce

qu'elle me masque mieux et qu'elle distance davantage le lecteur,"[1] and describes his *Jürg Jenatsch* as
"une espèce de fresque assez grossièrement dessinée
et pour être vue à distance."[2] He likes to stand apart
from his heroes, quite removed, to get the proper
distance and perspective, and apparently wants to
keep his readers away not only from himself but also
from his characters. So the frame-story becomes a
favorite form for his prose narratives,[3] since it removes the subjects as far as possible from the eye and
mitigates the harshness of the facts: "Die Neigung
zum Rahmen dann ist bei mir ganz instinctiv. Ich
halte mir den Gegenstand gerne vom Leibe oder
richtiger gerne so weit als möglich vom Auge und
dann will mir scheinen, das indirecte der Erzählung
(und selbst die Unterbrechungen) mildern die Härte
der Fabel."[4]

In four of his most artistic stories, *Der Heilige*,
Plautus im Nonnenkloster, *Das Leiden eines Knaben*,
Die Hochzeit des Mönchs, Meyer makes use of this
frame-form, which serves to assure him the character-
istics he considered dear, — formal restraint, calm se-
renity, cold objectivity, — as if he really should be
described in the phrase of Louise von François, who
called him "einen Telescopisten in Gegensatz zu
Ihrem Landsmann Keller, den ich einen Mikroscopi-
sten der Gegenwart nenne."[5] To this same correspond-
ent Meyer confesses, "Meine Lyrik, liebe Freundin,
verachte ich . . . weil sie mir . . . *nicht wahr genug*

erscheint. *Wahr* kann man (oder wenigstens ich) nur unter der dramatischen Maske al fresco sein. Im *Jenatsch* und im *Heiligen* . . . ist in den verschiedensten Verkleidungen weit mehr von mir, meinen wahren *Leiden und Leidenschaften,* als in dieser Lyrik, die kaum mehr als ein Spiel oder höchstens die Aeusserung einer untergeordneten Seite meines Wesens ist."[1] The section of his poems which might most readily be suspected of personal confession because of its title *Liebe,* begins with the poem *Alles war ein Spiel,* which warns the reader not to look in these lyrics for earnest purpose, amorous reminiscences, or expression of personal emotions requiring sympathy:

> Und ob verstohlen auf ein Blatt
> Auch eine Thräne fiel,
> Getrocknet ist die Thräne längst,
> Und alles war ein Spiel.[2]

In *Zur neuen Auflage* he wrote, to be sure,

> Was da steht, ich hab' es tief empfunden
> Und es bleibt ein Stück von meinem Leben — [3]

but he has concealed all personal allusions as much as possible, preferring not to reveal himself to the reader.

As he withdraws from his verses,[4] so he holds himself aloof from his stories, never clearly intruding his personal feeling or expressing his own opinion.[5] He views the characters he creates with the same objectivity with which his Michel Angelo stands in contemplation before his statues:

Ihr stellt des Leids Gebärde dar,
Ihr meine Kinder, ohne Leid!
So sieht der freigewordne Geist
Des Lebens überwundne Qual.
Was martert die lebend'ge Brust,
Beseligt und ergötzt im Stein.[1]

Like the statues of Michel Angelo, symbols of pent-up
energy under check and control:

Du packst mit nerv'ger Hand den Bart,
Doch springst du, Moses, nicht empor,

Meyer's men and women seem marble forms cut by a
sculptor from the stone, resembling the firm, plastic
figures of sculpture, the most objective of the arts.
Meyer, raising himself above base realities and still
baser passions to sublime and tragic heights, remains
objective and aloof in contemplation of them, cold,
calm, passionless, as if he lacked emotion. "Leiden-
schaftslosigkeit war ein Grundzug seines Wesens"[2] is
Frey's statement concerning him. For the misery of
his characters he apparently has only the cold words
of comfort of the Abu-Mohammed-al-Tabîb of his
story, "Es thut nicht weh" or "Es geht vorüber."[3]
They move him not: "Doch der Marmor fühlte
nichts,"[4] not even by death: "Und sterbt ihr, sterbt
ihr ohne Tod."[5]

As in the poem just cited, *Michel Angelo und seine
Statuen*, so in many others Meyer treats subjects derived from plastic or pictorial art, as the titles indicate: *Nach einem venezianischen Bild, Der römische*

Brunnen, Vor einer Büste, Das Gemälde, Der Marmorknabe, Das Münster, Nach einem Niederländer, Die gegeisselte Psyche, In der Sistina. .... In his stories, as well as in his verses, he uses frequent references to literary and especially pictorial and plastic art for illustration and comparison.[1] He describes life at the court of Navarra with words borrowed from an artist's vocabulary:

> An dem kleinen Hofe von Navarra
> War das Leben eine lose *Fabel*,
> Eine droh'nde oder heitre *Maske*
> Eine überraschende *Novelle*
> Ein phantastisch wahrheitloses *Schauspiel*.[2]

He derives his inspiration for his literary work very often from art [3] rather than reality, even remarking to Frey, "Lange, lange, war mir alles, was Wirklichkeit heisst, so zuwider als möglich."[4]

This dislike of reality and preference for art as a fairly secure refuge from life become a real danger for Meyer's literary work. This danger is increased by other qualities characteristic of him. In addition to the spirit of artistic restraint there is a tremendous aristocratic reserve in his personal bearing and his patrician outlook on life. The "odi profanum vulgus et arceo" of the ode of Horace becomes in Meyer's letters "Sie kennen mich und wissen, dass sich etwas in mir sträubt gegen die Betastungen der Menge."[5] He prefers, like his Poggio, to write for circles "wo die leiseste Anspielung verstanden ... wird."[6] His poems

are, in the phrase of a friend, "lauter Aristokraten-
kinder, d. h., zur Freude nur eines sehr auserlesenen
Publicums bestimmt."¹ He was conscious of this restricted appeal of his works to a selected public, con-
fiding in a visitor, "Man sollte eigentlich nichts vor-
aussetzen und allverständlich schreiben. Ich werd es
auch künftig tun. Mein Traum, mein Sehnen ist,
einmal ein Werk zu schreiben, das für das Volk allverständlich ist."² This longing was never realized,
and Meyer was sensitive and sensible enough to
know it. To many his poems appear passionless and
cold, as if they resembled the excellent watches that
represent the mechanical and aesthetic triumphs of
his compatriots in being mechanisms, not organisms;
to others they give the impression of austere clarity
and formal elegance, which assure them a small but
select group of sympathetic readers.³

To sum up, then, we may say that by laboring with
his creations, by continually correcting, revising, al-
tering, polishing, improving the style, by means of
extremely careful workmanship, Conrad Ferdinand
Meyer gives to his prose as well as to his verse an air
of solemn dignity, urbane polish, aristocratic elegance. His art appears impressive because of its
plastic objectivity, its classic restraint, its monumental grandeur. One discovers in his German works
the concreteness and precision which is of France, the
symmetry and order which is of Rome, the formal
beauty and flawless perfection which are customarily

considered more characteristic of Southern than of Northern art.[1] By studying Meyer's style, by examining his language in an attempt to discover the principles guiding him in the selection and arrangement of words by which he attained precision, plasticity, concentration, and nobility of expression in his poetry and prose, we may arrive at an understanding of the style and of the man. In solving the secret of his style, we can perhaps explain the problem of the enigmatic personality of Conrad Ferdinand Meyer.[2]

II

THE GRAND STYLE AND MANNER

Den Sinn des Grossen raubt mir keiner mehr.

GROSSER Styl, Grosse Kunst, all mein Denken und Träumen liegt darin."[1] Even if Meyer had not confessed to his publisher that his constant thought and dream was the attainment of the grand style and the grand manner in his art, examination of the subject matter and stylistic treatment of his poetry and prose would easily have established this preference. In curious contrast to the smallness of his own time and country and the comparative insignificance of his position among his own townsmen and compatriots, Meyer ardently desired in his dreams and their realization in art association with spacious times and great personages, as if in compensation for what life had in reality denied him. In our general introduction we have had occasion to observe the refuge he found in art from the trivialities of ordinary existence, his marked preference for all that was grand, and his resultant interest in great historical tragedies for treatment in his works. Contrasting rather than relating life and art, he selected the past rather than the present as the setting and subject of his verses

and stories, and for characters preferred tragic
heroes of the great world to small, commonplace
people of his own time and social sphere.

The vocabulary of these heroes, who are the powers
on or behind the throne, Meyer could not very well
take from the ordinary speech of everyday conversation. He accordingly avoids colloquial words, common foreign terms, and the dialect expressions of provincial speech.[1] In order to elevate his language to
the level of his elegant heroes and their aristocratic
entourage, to suit his style to his subject matter,
Meyer quite regularly prefers, not only in his poetry[2]
but also in his prose,[3] the poetic word to the prosaic,
the unusual to the usual, the rare to the common, the
elegant to the unrefined, the urbane to the vulgar, the
noble and sublime expression to the one that is commonplace and banal.

Since his heroes all stand "auf hoher Stufe,"[4] — to
use a phrase from his verse, — they must all be, in
speech and in appearance, — to employ a phrase from
his stories, — "mit Wahl gekleidet, obschon im Rei-
segewand."[5] Meyer becomes, as a matter of fact, as
"wählerisch" as his Poggio, who avoids the uncouth
words of the barbaric novice whose story he relates
and substitutes for them more refined words of his
own cultivated choice.[6] Like his Dante, whom he
dares make the *raconteur* of another Renaissance
story, Meyer prefers to plead forgetfulness[7] or, like
his Faustine, to pause in silence[8] rather than to

offend our ears with unrefined words. When his characters stoop to vulgar speech they become apologetic
like Fagon.[1] For, like the Louis XIV of his story,
Meyer seems to have vowed never, not even in narrative, to let a word cross his lips that should seem ordinary or common or out of keeping with the character
of a king.[2] His vocabulary, therefore, carefully and
fastidiously chosen, is urbane, noble, courtly, even
regal in its solemn, dignified elegance and aristocratic
splendor.[3]

Meyer's characters, accordingly, have the manners
and vocabulary of refined intercourse. The ordinary
verb *gehen* gives way to the more elevated verbs
wallen, wandeln, wandern, schreiten: "Geht er, wunder-
licher nie / *Wallte* man auf Erden";[4] "Und sie *wandelt*
durch des Thores Wölbung / Und sie *wandelt* durch
die dunkeln Gassen."[5] "Ich *wandle* gern auf dieser
Erde"[6] is a characteristic expression for these people,
called "*wandellustig*,"[7] whose evening walk becomes
an "*Abendwandel*,"[8] for whom life seems, in fact,
"ein flücht'ger *Wandel*."[9] "Zu *wandern* ist das Herz
verdammt,"[10] writes Meyer, but not only the human
heart wanders in his verses, "kleebeladene Kamele
wandern."[11] Like *wallen* and *wandern*, there occur frequently *schleichen*, *pilgern*, and *irren*: "Kutscher, du
schleichst wie eine Schnecke";[12] "Weiter *pilgernd*,
rätselt' ich ein Weilchen";[13] "Jüngst *irrt*' ich traurig
und allein."[14]

The verb *schreiten* gives the best illustration of the

nobility which these verbs lend to Meyer's elevated style. We find in the poems, for example:

> Sie hebt die erste sich, erweckt die Schnitterschar,
> Ergreift die blanke Sichel, die im Schatten lag,
> Und *schreitet* herrlich durch das Goldgewog des Korns,
> Umblaut vom Himmel, als ein göttliches Gebild.[1]

> In der Faust zerrissne Ketten,
> *Schreit'* ich durch des Hades Nacht! [2]

> Sie *schreitet* in bacchisch bevölkertem Raum
> Mit wehenden Haaren ein glühender Traum.[3]

> Rief mordend aus: "Ich bad' in Tau!"
> Und *schritt* in roten Bächen.[4]

> *Schreitend* mit dem Lenz und seinen Flöten,
> *Schreitend* durch die Sommerabendröten. . . .
> Rastlos *schreitend* ohne Ziel und Ende! . . .
> Bin ich der zum *Reiseschritt* Verdammte![5]

In the stories, we read: "Er [der Rappe des Pescara] schnoberte, als wittere er schon den Pulverdampf und *schritt* stolz als trage er den Sieg";[6] "Wie sich der Rauch verzog, lag das Feld mit Spaniern bedeckt, zwischen Todten und Verwundeten *schritt* Pescara."[7]

At times the verb *schreiten*, so frequently used,[8] seems somewhat absurd; we are informed, for example, that even sparrows and finches stride about: "Und durch die Gitterstäbe *schritten* / Sperling und Fink mit freien Sitten."[9] With one of Meyer's characters we might exclaim, "Wie schlank sie *schreiten*!"[10] without doing violence to his usage, which permits "Wir *schreiten* schlank und jung,"[11] and even "In wilden Gruppen *schritten* eilig sie."[12] Sheer physical

discomfort does not seem to deter these hardy heroes
from their majestic stride. Thus in *Jürg Jenatsch*,
"drehte sich [die Unterredung] um das Ausschneiden
von Leichdornen. Erinnert Euch, dass Ihr über den
Obersten gespottet habt, als er vor ein paar Tagen
mit einem Pantoffel am linken Fusse *einherschritt*."[1]
Even widows and orphans, wailing in lamentation, do
not lose their bearing: "Witwen, Waisen *schreiten*
jammernd."[2] They may, of course, like Cäsar Borgia
in the poem bearing his name, *Cäsar Borjas Ohnmacht*, cry out as they walk, "Ich *schreite* ... qualvoll
... doch ich *schreite*."[3]

As Meyer prefers *schreiten* to the less distinctive
verb *gehen*, so he prefers *lauschen* to the less elegant
horchen: "... eine gafft / Lüstern, eine sinnt dämonenhaft / Eine *lauscht* mit hartem Mördersinn."[4]
This elevated verb is common in his poems [5] and in
his prose.[6] In a moment of tense emotional excitement it is sometimes used to achieve a fine dramatic
climax for a chapter's close, as at the end of the first
chapter of *Pescara*: "Er ist unter uns und *lauscht*!
schrie der Herzog mit gellender Stimme."[7]

Lugen and *spähen* are for similar effect substituted
for *schauen*: "Und *lugte* sorgend zu den Wolken auf";[8]
"Sie *spähen* durch die Hallen."[9] Meyer likewise prefers *weisen* to *zeigen*: "Und er *wies* auf ein Gelände."[10]

When Meyer's heroes succumb to the common
physical pangs of hunger and thirst they do so only
in ultra-refined, fastidious fashion, expressed by the

verbs *lechzen, darben*: "Der üpp'ge Mund, indem er *lechzt*";[1] "Sie sieht mich dursten, *lechzen, darben.*"[2] In similar fastidious fashion these august heroes appease their bodily desires by *nippen, schlürfen*: "Statt milden Nektars, Rebenblut / Geruhten sie zu *nippen*";[3] "Es schaudert. Einen vollen Becher fasst / Es gierig noch und *schlürft* in toller Hast";[4] "*Lechzend* öffnet' ich das Fenster, / *Einzuschlürfen* Morgenlüfte."[5] At a wedding breakfast in Meyer's stories, "*schlürft* [man] Cybrier und verzehrt als Hochzeitsgepäcke die Amarellen."[6]

Meyer's heroes, aristocratic but sturdy, who yield to thirst and hunger with restraint, endure physical pain in similar manner, not crying out — to recall Lessing — like Philoctetes in the drama or Laokoön of Vergil's poem, but merely sighing, like the Laokoön of the famous statue, in the verbs *seufzen, keuchen, stöhnen*: "'Jetzt nenne mir deine Gottheit!' flehte Victoria. 'Ich beschwöre dich, Pescara, nenne sie mir!' 'Ich glaube, da ist sie selbst,' *keuchte* er heiser. Immer schwerer begann er zu athmen, er *stöhnte*, er *ächzte*, er röchelte."[7] It is characteristic to have heroes appear "Mit *lechzender* Zunge, / Mit *keuchender* Lunge,"[8] to indulge in *seufzen*,[9] *keuchen*,[10] *stöhnen*.[11]

When these heroes finally laugh they do not indulge in a mere plebeian *lachen*: "Guicciardin schlug eine fröhliche *Lache* auf";[12] "Und Strozzis *Lache* dröhnte."[13]

We are not surprised therefore to find changes as commonplace as the lighting, extinguishing, and dying down of a candle described in Meyer's verses in the following elevated terms: "Die eine Kerze flammt er an . . . eine Kerze haucht er aus";[1] "Er löscht die Fackel. Sie verloht."[2] Just as simple prose sentences like "Du hattest Tränen im Auge" read in Meyer "Die *Zähre* die dir an der *Wimper* quoll,"[3] so "durstig trank er aus einer Quelle" is transformed into "Doch wo er *lechzend schlürft'* aus einem *Quell*."[4] When Meyer's characters of heroic stature and tragic mien drink they sometimes sip from a *Becher*,[5] a *Kelch*,[6] or *Pokal*,[7] but more commonly and by preference, "feierlich aus voller *Schale*":[8] "Dann füllt ein jeder seine *Schale* sich / Mit duft'gem Wein und schlürft und keiner darbt!";[9] "Kreisend durch die Reiche sah ich glänzen / Eine *Schale*, draus ein jedes trank."[10] Not enough that it be a *Schale*, it must be nobly wrought: "[Poggio] hob eine edle von einem lachenden Satyr umklammerte *Schale*."[11]

As the favorite drinking vessel is the *Schale*, so the favorite mode of lighting is the *Ampel*. Occasionally Meyer does not spurn the ordinary lamp. In *Jürg Jenatsch* we find an "italienische eiserne *Oellampe*" burning, as it were, in unabashed simplicity.[12] But when it better suits his purpose the *Oellampe* suddenly becomes an *Ampel* on the same page. "Da stürzte plötzlich die *Ampel* klirrend auf den Boden und *verglomm*. Ein Schuss war durch das Fenster gefallen." Similarly in *Pescara* we do not find, at the end of chapter iv, the phrase "Dann ging das Licht aus," but instead the nicely calculated close "Dann *erlosch die Ampel.*"[1] So we find his heroine "Victoria Colonna, das Weib des Pescara und die Perle Italiens . . . bei der keuschen *Ampel* in Italiens grosse Dichter vertieft,"[2] his hero Thomas Becket writing "bei dem gleichmässig milden Scheine einer griechischen *Ampel,*"[3] and Michel Angelo sitting "in wachem Traum, / Umhellt von einer kleinen *Ampel* Brand."[4] The opposite of "Tageslicht" in Meyer's terminology is "*Ampelschein*";[5] in his poems[6] as in his prose[7] "brennt die *Ampel* im Gemach."[8] One poem, indeed, is entitled "Die *Ampel.*"[9]

When a character seeks rest he spurns the ordinary *Bett*: "Schlummernd sinkt er auf das *Lager*";[10] more often the couch he seeks is the *Pfühl*: "Er steht an ihrem *Pfühl* in herber Qual,"[11] even though sometimes it be of stone,[12] or merely a hard seat in a boat: "Aus der Schiffsbank mach' ich meinen *Pfühl.*"[13]

When these characters dress they don a mantle, which is a favorite garb with Meyer as with Grillparzer. So we read of "den blauen langen *Mantel*" of Charlemagne[14] or of Pescara; "Der Helm war ihm vom Kopfe gerissen und sein dunkler *Mantel* flatterte zerfetzt."[15] Often the mantle is *der Purpur*:[16] "Statt des *Purpurs* trug er schlichtes Reis'gewand"[17] is a fact worthy of mention, for ordinarily the characters are dressed in the robes of state which befit them and desire, even when troubled, that their torments be appropriately cloaked: "über meine Qualen wirfst du würdevolle *Purpurfalten*."[1]

Where ordinary mortals merely walk softly, Meyer's men and women tread "auf stillen *Sohlen*,"[2] "auf nackten *Sohlen*."[3] Meyer's Victoria Colonna steps "auf leisen *Sohlen*";[4] his Poggio boasts, "Ich schmeichle mir in den meinigen [Schriften] mit leichten *Sohlen* zu schreiten."[5] Elsewhere in Meyer's works[6] *Sohlen* is used even to absurd extremes: "Schritte fühlend hinter ihren *Sohlen*."[7] For the ordinary "Ich mache mich auf den Weg" or "auf die Füsse" he prefers "Ich mache selbst mich auf die *Sohlen*."[8]

Not content with walking simply on their feet, as we have seen, these characters in riding similarly scorn the common *Pferd*. Instead they are mounted on a *Ross*,[9] *Gaul*,[10] *Renner*,[11] or, like Thomas Becket and Angela Borgia, "auf einem schneeweissen *Zelter*."[12]

When not mounted they prefer *die Sänfte* to all other means of conveyance on land, a preference not wholly to be explained away as an attempt at historical accuracy. "Holt mir eine *Sänfte*," calls Kaiser Sigmund,[13] and he is not alone among Meyer's characters in this demand. Pescara orders both his *Sänfte* and his *Rappen* for his final expedition, letting the impulse of the last moment decide between them.[14] That this is due to a fastidiousness of choice on

Meyer's part is shown by the frequency with which the word occurs,[1] and by the fact that on water these characters ride in a *Barke*[2] in preference to any other craft, with a *Ferge*[3] as their favorite oarsman.

As for personal appearance, we can hardly expect these heroes to have ordinary *Haar*, simple and unadorned. It is at least *Ringelhaar*,[4] or *Kraushaar*,[5] or referred to as *Locken*[6] or *Gelock*.[7] "Und ob die *Locke* mir ergraut"[8] is the approved manner of expressing approaching old age.

In his choice of adjectives, as in his choice of verbs and nouns, Meyer follows the same principles of selection, preferring the unusual word to the ordinary, the noble, elevated epithet to the terms of colloquial discourse. For *alt* and *krank* we find *greis*[9] and *siech*:[10] in *Hutten*, "Eins bist du: *Siech*";[11] in *Pescara*, "Und da deine *greisen* und *siechen* Eltern in Tricarico darben";[12] in the poems, "Deine *greisen* Eltern darben."[13]

The same festive splendor is manifest in Meyer's selection of aristocratic adjectives of color. What more fitting than that these characters, lords and ladies all, clad in brocade and ermine, should be mantled in *red* and decked with *gold*: "Zwölf junge Gondoliere und Pagen in *Roth* und *Gold*, die Farben des Herzogs,"[14] which appear also to be the colors of Meyer. "Mich lüstet nach dem *rothen* Kleid,"[15] cries a character, voicing the sentiments of all. Pescara appears "in flammend *rothem* Kleid,"[16] Jürg Jenatsch "in einem *Scharlachkleide*,"[1] as "der Reiter in *Scharlach*,"[2] "in *Scharlach* gekleidet,"[3] "in juwelenglänzender *rother* Tracht,"[4] choosing *roth*[5] as his favorite color.

Meyer, like Schiller,[6] is fond of the royal *purpurn*[7] and of the poetic *golden*.[8] He likes to combine the two, *roth* and *gold*. A publisher binding his books in red and adorning them with gold, the colors of the old Haessel edition, which has long remained the standard, shows sympathetic appreciation of him and his art.

There is a marked fondness for golden hair, designated as *blond*.[9] "Die *Blonde* mit dem roten Sammtgewande,"[10] "ein hell Geschöpf in *sonnenlichten* Flechten"[11] are typical figures with Meyer. This typical figure, clad in red, with hair of gold, has eyes of blue;[12] with "Des Nackens *Blond*gekraus" goes "Des Augen tiefes *Blau*,"[13] "Durch weisse Lider schimmert *blaues* Licht."[14] *Roth, gold, blau* are Meyer's colors, the colors of bright pageantry, of pomp and circumstance, of festive state and splendor. Thus Jürg Jenatsch appears, "der Schimmer eines *Scharlachkleides* und eine hochragende *blaue* Hutfeder";[15] "Voran auf einem schwarzen Hengst ein Reiter in *Scharlach*, von dessen Stülphute *blaue* Federn wehten, der jedem Kinde bekannte Jürg Jenatsch."[16] Blue[17] is the predominant color for the water and the sky: "Das leuchtende *Blau* des himmlischen Tages";[18] "O *blaue* Flut."[19] Meyer's zeal to select the unusual and

give it currency by frequent use possibly leads him to
the word *fahl* and its variant *falb*.[1]

To employ the terminology established by investigation of adjectives of color in literary documents,[2]
we may say that Meyer in general employs the decided colors of the "classic" writers; there is in his
writings no "romantic" riot of color, no "romantic"
tendency toward accurate and subtle distinction of
color with a fondness for unusual contrasts and combinations which result in some moderns in oriental
warmth, in others in repellent decadence. Meyer
resembles Shakspere, Schiller, and Hebbel in his fondness for red, which "persists as the most popular color
with the poets."[3] Red, gold, blue are his favorite decided colors; brown,[4] green,[5] black,[6] white,[7] grey [8] also
occur in his works; yellow [9] is rarely employed; mention of a shade like violet [10] is almost unique. Meyer's
Farbenlust, of which he speaks,[11] is marked, therefore,
but restricted, illustrating the chaste reserve, the
aristocratic restraint, and the spirit of festive elegance
which we have come to recognize as characteristic of
him and his art.

Meyer frequently elevates and ennobles the adjective by raising it to the rank of a noun. The substantive use of the adjective is a common poetic device
which Bodmer praised in Milton and recommended
for German poets, who, from Klopstock down, have
regularly employed it in their verses. It is not uncommon in German prose, but rarely so frequent as in

Meyer. Instead of the word *Hand* he prefers to be explicit: "Mit der *Rechten* kühn gerudert, / Doch in ausgestreckter *Linken*";[1] "Ihre Kniee fasst er mit der *Linken*, / In der *Rechten* droht des Schwertes Blinken";[2] "Die *Linke* um Victoria schlingend, er- griff er mit der *Rechten* die Hand Numas";[3] "in welcher der Primas mit der ängstlichen *Linken* zu- rücknahm, was seine grossmüthige *Rechte* gegeben."[4] This use of *die Rechte*[5] and *die Linke*[6] is so frequent as to require comment. More extraordinary is the laconic solemnity and monumental grandeur of effect[7] of majestic combinations like the following: "Nur ein *Sorgloser*, ein *Fahrlässiger*, ein *Pflichtverges- sener* . . . verschiebe und versäume es";[8] "Blicke ich wie eine *Leidenschaftliche* und *Leichtfertige?*";[9] "War er nicht der *Starke* und *Freie*, der *Fröhliche* und *Zuversichtliche*, der dem Feinde ins Auge sah?"; [10] "Es ist nur, damit er mich nicht für eine *Leichtfertige* halte und für eine *Undankbare*";[11] "Aber ich frage mich, ob es gut sei, die *Verschmähte* an einen *Herz- losen* und *Grausamen* zu fesseln";[12] "und er wäre ein *Abscheulicher* gewesen."[13]

As the three women who have forged the chains of Italy are pictured by Morone, Victoria exclaims in turn: "*Die Schändliche! . . . Aermste . . . Unse- lige!*"[14] When Meyer's characters cry out in reproach or criticism or blame, their form of address is the ad- jective dignified into a noun: "ich *Zager*";[15] "du

Stolzer!";[1] "du *Ueberkluger!*";[2] "du *Arge!*";[3] "*Böse!*";[4] "Gieb Antwort, *Grausamer!*"[5] In positions of emphasis like this, the substantive form of the adjective is apt; also at the end of a sentence: "Kommen werde ich als die, welche ich mich nenne, und welche ich bin! *die Unberührte, die Jungfräuliche*";[6] or at the close of a chapter: "Und *der Listige* trat in die Nacht zurück, die sich inzwischen auf die ewige Stadt gesenkt hatte."[7]

By dignifying the adjective to a noun Meyer attains considerable nobility of expression. He avoids using the adjective by so turning it into a noun or by letting a noun take its place.[8] He writes to Rodenberg of his purpose in writing *Die Richterin*, "soviel ich vermag, ohne Adjektive,"[9] and he succeeds, as Borries, Freiherr von Münchhausen has pointed out, in writing his ballad entitled *Mit zwei Worten* with only two epithets, "mit zwei Beiworten."[10] He is extremely sparing in his use of epithets, commonly employing only one before a noun, and then by preference a simple one. He seems to have rediscovered the beauty of the short monosyllabic adjective and to have solved the secret of dignifying this simple epithet by letting it stand alone in solitary isolation before its noun.[11] Monosyllabic adjectives seem most common among Meyer's epithets: "und seine *bangen* Blicke befragten das *zarte* Haupt auf dem *blassen* Goldgrunde"; [12]

> Lebet wohl, ihr *grellen* Hirtenflöten,
> Um die Gunst der *jungen* Corsin werbend!
> Lebet wohl, ihr *warmen* Abendröten,
> In den *weiten* Himmeln selig sterbend.[1]

From comparatively simple words like *frisch, jung, schön, süss, tief, voll, warm, weit,* which seem to enjoy special favor with Meyer,[2] and which have no special grandeur of meaning or form to recommend them, he sometimes secures startling and tremendous effect, approaching on occasion the sublime: "Dass ich einem ganzen *vollen* Glücke / *Stillen* Kuss auf *stumme* Lippen drücke";[3] "Sie hebt das *volle* Glas mit *nacktem* Arm";[4]

> Und wo der Purpur flatternd fliegt,
> Sprühn Funken, lodern Flammen auf!
> Der Corse fährt aus seinem Traum
> Und starrt in Moskaus *weiten* Brand.[5]

At times Meyer makes the most of a common word by employing it in an elevated sense, for example the word *frech,* which occurs frequently in his works:[6] "Ich freute mich der *frechen* Jugendthat";[7] "So *grelle* und *freche* Worte redete die Richterin";[8] "in *nackten frechen* Armen."[9] Section VII of the *Gedichte* he entitles "*Frech* und *Fromm.*" Similar is Meyer's use of *wild,* which is even more common in occurrence:[10] "In deiner *wilden* Scheu"[11] raises the common word *wild,* like *frech* above, to the rank of a poetic epithet.

The same Meyer who commonly uses simple monosyllables and prefers the single epithet, scolds a
character in one of his stories "für eine ellenlange
Phrase,"[1] and takes her to task for her tendency to
ornate style which makes her hang "ihre blanke
Natur aus reiner Angst mit dem Lumpen einer ge-
flickten Phrase,"[2] pointing out to her that "der
botanische Garten ist kurzweg der botanische Garten" and not what she would make of it with her
"weitläufigen verblühten Rhetorik."[3]

Meyer was himself somewhat fastidious in the selection of the single epithet which he usually employs,[4] often rejecting, as his manuscripts with their
variant readings show, half a dozen adjectives[5] before
he is satisfied that he has hit upon the "most
proper word in the most proper place,"[6] "le mot
juste"[7] which seems to him eminently appropriate.
The same careful restraint and aristocratic reserve
which keep him from heaping epithet on epithet in
the manner of some poets[8] keep him from using
many new epithets of his own devising,[9] resplendent
with novel brilliance like those compounded by
Heine, Kleist, and Mörike. Certainly his sensitive
nature shrank from the ostentatious immodesty manifest in the neologisms in the poetry of Detlev von
Liliencron.[10] He frequently performed the more difficult task of elevating common words to distinction in
his style. His poetry, however, as I have elsewhere
pointed out,[11] regularly utilizes the conventional po-

etic vocabulary; he makes much use of rare and poetical words in both his poetry and his prose.[1]

In addition to the simple monosyllables of common speech which he ennobles by his use, not unlike Rainer Maria Rilke among the moderns, Meyer also employs epithets dignified in meaning and form. At times he even seems to share the fondness of Schiller and Klopstock[2] for the participle, past and present, as epithet:

> *Sprengende* Reiter und *flatternde* Blüten,
> Einer voraus mit *gescheitelten* Locken —
> Ist es der Lenz auf *geflügeltem* Renner?
> *Jubelnde* Gassen und *jubelnde* Wimpel
> Und ein von *treibender* Jugend *geschwelltes*
> *Jubelndes* Herz in dem Busen des Stuart.[3]

Even an insensitive listener is impressed by the metrical effect of these participles, the acoustical quality of the initial combination "ju," recurring four times.[4] In this poem of forty-one lines, *Die Rose von Newport*, the present participle occurs sixteen times as epithet, the past participle eight. Similarly, in the eighteen lines of *Der Botenlauf*, which begins

> Blicke gen Himmel gewandt, *gebreitete flehende* Arme!
> Murmeln und *schallender* Ruf *knieender* Mädchen und
>   Frau'n,[5]

the past participle occurs four times, the present ten. The proportion is striking, thirty-two participles in forty-one lines, fourteen in eighteen.

The use of the participle often lends dignity: "Ein stilles, scheues, *ungezähmtes* Kind";[1] "mit *allumarmender* Gebärde";[2] "'S ist Klio, die das Altertum *enträtselnde*";[3] or it makes for concentration: "Ein schlankes Mädchen zielt mit *rückgebognem* Arm, / In *schwachgeballter* Faust den *unbesiegten* Speer."[4]

There is considerable dignity also, both in meaning and form, to some of the adjectives ending in "ig" which Meyer is uncommonly fond of using with the "i" usually elided,[5] e. g. *ew'ger, heil'ger, mächt'ger. Ewig,*[6] *gewaltig,*[7] *heilig,*[8] *mächtig,*[9] *nervig*[10] are frequently found. The dignified, sonorous effect is apparent in forms like "ein *leichtsinniges* Gesind,"[11] "ein fein, *halsstarrig* Weib,"[12] or when one addresses Achilles "unter deinem *mächt'gen* Augenlid!"[13] or describes Michel Angelo's Moses, "Du packst mit *nerv'ger* Hand den Bart,"[14] or finds Michel Angelo himself "In der Sistine dämmerhohem Raum, / Das Bibelbuch in seiner *nerv'gen* Hand."[15]

There is similar dignity attaching to the meaning and form of certain adjectives ending in "isch," which is apparent in "ein *verführerisches* Bildnis," [16] "jene *prahlerischen* Knaben," [17] "mit *dämonischen* Gesichten";[18] to adjectives ending in "los": *schlummerlos,*[19] *gedankenlos,*[20] and so on;[21] to those ending in "voll": *ahnungsvoll,*[22] *geheimnisvoll*;[23] to those ending in "haft": *launenhaft,*[24] *dämonenhaft*;[25] also to forms like *unvergleichlich,*[26] *unsagbar,*[27] as in the conclusion to *Cäsar Borjas Ohnmacht*: "Aus allen Wänden quillt es schwarz hervor / Und dunkelt über mir . . . *Unsagbar* Graun. . . ."

Meyer knew the value of epithets like *ekel,*[1] *frevel,*[2] *grausam,*[3] *lüstern:*[4] "einen *eklen* Knäuel,"[5] "mit *frevler* Faust,"[6] "ein *grausam lüstern* Spiel,"[7] "ein *erhabener* Zorn — eine *grossartige* Sünderin — Ein *gewaltiges* Weib von *furchtbarer* Schönheit,"[8] "auf seiner *mächtigen* Stirn, auf den *magern* Händen traten die *blauen* Adern hervor und ein *furchtbarer* Ernst sprach aus seiner Miene."[9] *Ahnungsvoll, dämonenhaft, erhaben, frevel, furchtbar, gewaltig, grausam, grossartig, mächtig, ungeheuer, wunderbar* in both meaning and form are sonorous and majestic epithets, which Meyer fully exploited to attain the grand manner.

It is a common practice nowadays to characterize a famous author by his favorite epithet.[10]   We may recognize Klopstock in his *inbrünstig, göttlich, heilig, olympisch, ätherisch;* Heine in his *still, heimlich, einsam, seltsam, dunkel;* the "Storm and Stress" writers in *unendlich, überschwenglich, göttlich, schrecklich;* young Goethe in *golden, munter;* old Goethe in *geistreich, anständig, bedeutend, ewig,*[11] and so on.[12]   So Korrodi finds "Lieblingsadjektive der verhaltenen Natur Meyers sind rein und keusch."[13]   In the same category with *rein*[14] and *keusch,*[15] he might have included *kühl,*[16] *scheu,*[17] *schlank,*[18] *zart,*[19] some of which occur even more commonly and are quite as characteristic of him.

It is likewise normal for Meyer, whose adjectives of color we have already noticed, to appeal to the sense of sight with *blank*,[1] *blass*,[2] *bleich*,[3] *dunkel*,[4] *düster*,[5] *hell*,[6] *licht*,[7] and to the sense of hearing with *dumpf*,[8] *leis*,[9] *sacht*,[10] and *still*,[11] for he wrote not only for the eye but also for the ear. Like Goethe, who remarked, "Freilich ist die Poesie nicht fürs Auge gemacht,"[12] or Shakspere, who "loved words for their sound, and not for their sense alone,"[13] or other authors, whom Stevenson selects as seemingly so fond of certain tonal effects that they are probably unaware "of the length to which they push this melody of letters,"[14] Meyer was inordinately fond of certain combinations of vowels and consonants in words which seem to suit the mouth and please the ear. Among the epithets already mentioned which may have been chosen for their marked tonal appeal may be enumerated the following: *ekel, frech, frevel, gell, graus, grausam, grausig, greis, grell, herb, jäh, keck, kraus, nervig, wild, wund, wunderbar, wunderlich, wundersam, zäh*, the sound of which is more striking in combination with other words, as for example: "Die *grause* Larve,"[15] "Es zuckt in *grauser* Lust,"[16] "dieses *grause* Lastern,"[17] "das *grause* Haupt,"[18] "ein *grauser* Wetterschlag."[19] Perhaps similar considerations of sound attracted Meyer to verbs like *dröhnen, gellen, lodern, lohen, peitschen, quellen, zucken*, which occur frequently in his works.[20]

"Die Romanen scheinen ein schärferes Ohr zu

haben für die Klangwerte der Sprache, während um-
gekehrt die Germanen . . . sich selten so am blossen
Wortklang berauschen," thinks Müller-Freienfels.[1]
It is possible that Meyer, who confesses to having
been French for ten years of his life and to possessing,
as a result, a preference "für die rein stilistischen
Vorzüge der französischen Literatur,"[2] did not read
the literature in which Victor Hugo plays so important a part without acquiring "das französische
Ohr," which he attributes to himself.[3] Certainly his
ear was delicately attuned to the pitch and quantity
of vowels and extremely sensitive to the character of
consonants. In featuring the highly developed visualizing powers of Meyer and his characters, who, like
their creator, accurately remember scenes which they
portray, we are prone to forget that at least one
among them, Morone, was possessed of a very acute
ear and a highly developed auditory memory as well.
Only recall the line, "[Morone] setzte diese Scene
fort, jedes Wort des Zwiegesprächs *wiederholte sich in
seinem Ohr.*"[4] Possibly Meyer was accustomed to
doing the same. Certainly he was very different in
this respect from Gottfried Keller, who said, "Das
Ohr kann bei mir nichts tun, da ich von Anfang an
weder für mich allein laut las, was ich geschrieben,
noch jemals eine Umgebung hatte, der ich etwas vor-
lesen konnte oder mochte," and who produced, on
that account, poems which are "nicht gehört, sondern
gedacht."[5] As a matter of fact, Meyer made a confession which is almost exactly opposed to Keller's.

In conversation with Kögel he remarked, "Es ist mir nicht zu entbehrendes Bedürfnis geworden, alles nach aussen hin schaubar, sichtbar zu gestalten, auch in der Sprache, den Accenten"; [1] and Kalischer, stressing this last phrase, "in der Sprache, den Accenten," thinks, "So ist damit gesagt, dass er die Wirkung, die er ausüben will, schon von der Art der Zusammenstellung der Worte als eines akustischen Materials abhängig machen wollte."[2] Korrodi shows "[wie Meyer] mählich seine Rede nach Herders Gebot 'tönen' hörte, wie er diktando immer mehr die akustische Wirkung des geschriebenen Wortes bedachte."[3] Wüst explains how often "der Dichter [Meyer] bei seiner Wortwahl die Musik gradezu anruft,"[4] and Schollenberger emphasizes "die grosse akustische Wirkung . . . die das ganze Antlitz seiner Dichtung auch der Lyrik (bisweilen!) bestimmt."[5]

Many modern critics emphasize the tonal effect of poetry above all else, grouping *Dichtkunst* with *Tonkunst* and *Raumkunst* as *Wortkunst*,[6] as if Hamlet's reply to the query of Polonius, "What do you read, my lord?" "Words, words, words," had acquired an altogether new significance, universal in its application. Max Dessoir, for example, formulates "die Kronprinzenwahrheit, der die Zukunft gehört; an den Wort- und Satzvorstellungen selber haftet der Genuss,"[7] and German[8] and American[9] investigations concentrate on establishing this melody of letters in different literary documents, and even conclude with the ambitious formulation "that each poet, whether consciously or not, had secured a certain definite tonal effect, a tonality, if you will, by the way his sounds were combined, and that this tonal effect was the chief sensational contribution to the esthetic enjoyment of his verse."[1]

Without setting out to prove the tonal effect of Meyer's poetry by any such elaborate laboratory investigations, without even proceeding on the principle that "heard melodies are sweet, but those unheard are sweeter," we can prove Meyer's interest in sound more simply by citing his love of alliteration: "*S*achte *Sch*ritt er, *Sch*läfrig *Sch*leift er, / Wie Ge-*Sch*lurfe von Pantoffeln."[2] The poem *Venedigs erster Tag*[3] opens with a line in "g," "Eine *G*lück *G*efüllte *G*ondel *G*leitet auf dem Canal *G*rande," continues with this line in "r," "*R*ings in Stücke sp*R*ang ze*R*-schmette*R*t *R*omas *R*ost'ge *R*iesenkette," and elsewhere fairly teems with alliterative phrases.

Meyer's poems are meant to be read aloud so that one can appreciate the sonorous title *Lenz Wanderer, Mörder, Triumphator,*[4] the majestic sweep of the line "*Unbevölkert flutet eine schrankenlose Wasserbreite,*"[5] or the stanza, which Moser finds one unfamiliar with German would feel to be written in the language of Dante,[6]

> Aus der Laube niederhangend,
> Glutdurchwogt und üppig rund,
> Schwebt' ich dunkelpurpurprangend
> Ueber einem roten Mund![7]

From these examples we readily realize why Meyer's verse as well as his prose gains on being read aloud, why Meyer's "Balladen zu den vortragbarsten Stücken der ganzen deutschen epischen Dichtung in gebundener Rede [zählen]," [1] and why "Eine Novelle wie *Die Hochzeit des Mönchs* aufmerksam, Satz für Satz *vor*gelesen werden [will]." [2]
His poems are excellently adapted for recitation because they combine sound and sense in dramatic form. His dramatic desires, which never resulted in a drama, [3] urged him to make his poems ever more dramatic and compact, as we can readily observe from a comparison of their early forms with the finished product. In the early version of his poems, *Romanzen und Bilder*, we are quite unmoved to read, for example,

> Ueber Leichen, grausig hingemäht,
> Steigt zum Kapitol er unverzagt.
> Wo in seiner Frevel Kreis er steht
> Die er alle haupthoch überragt. [4]

These lines should tell of the mad frenzy of Cäsar Borgia, who has drunk the poisoned cup and, with death already coursing through his veins, rushes to the capitol to claim the crown. Revision of the verses results in this much more dramatic description:

> Ich komme! Ich vertausendfache mich!
> Ich steige mordend auf das Kapitol
> Und mit Italiens Krone krön' ich mir
> Dies Haupt, das seine Frevel überragt! [5]

The same tendencies toward tonal effect and dramatic concentration are even more strikingly apparent in the finales of his poems.[1] It is especially interesting to observe how carefully Meyer calculates this closing note[2] and how his poems gain in dramatic vigor by culminating in a powerful climax. The poem *Die Karyatide*, which ended rather lamely in an early version, "Erwachend sah den Brand sie lohn und sann: / Es ist Paris . . . Sie morden sich,"[3] reads in its final form, "Sie gähnt' und blickte rings sich um: / Wo bin ich denn? In welcher Stadt? / Sie morden sich. Es ist Paris."[4] The improvement here is so manifest that it scarcely requires comment: her sleepy yawn after three hundred years of rest; her dull gaze of wonder at being so rudely disturbed; her surprised question when half awake, "Wo bin ich denn?"; her eyes opened wide, "In welcher Stadt?"; her resulting revulsion at the discovery, "Sie morden sich. Es ist Paris."

Sound and sense combine in magnificent climaxes like the following to give the effect of dramatic finality:

Den ersten Menschen formtest du aus Thon,
Ich werde schon von härterm Stoffe sein,
Da Meister, brauchst du deinen Hammer schon,
Bildhauer Gott, schlag' zu! Ich bin der Stein.[5]

Gelockt vom Rauschen einer überreifen Saat,
Wird sie zur starken Schnitterin. Die Sichel klingt.[6]

Ein Blitz. Zwei schwarze Rosse bäumen sich.
Die Peitsche knallt. Sie ziehen an. Vorbei.[7]

Wählst du dir solches? Nimm drei Tage Frist!
... Drei Tage Frist? Sie sind vorbei. Brich auf![1]

Sie schmiegt ihn um die blonden Haare leicht,
Sie steht bekränzt. Sie schaudert. Sie erbleicht.[2]

Sie liegt, den Hals gebogen, auf dem Rasen,
Sie hört die Hirtenflöte wieder blasen
Und lauscht. Sie zuckt. Sie windet sich. Sie ruht.[3]

Not only in the concluding line of a poem or in the close of a chapter is Meyer's aim to attain dramatic expression manifest, but throughout entire works of poetry and prose. This will perhaps be most satisfactorily proved by quoting from two of his poems, the first of which illustrates his attainment of nobility by the dignity of his adjectives, the second by the majesty of his verbs.

DIE *STERBENDE* MEDUSE

Ein *kurzes* Schwert gezückt in *nerv'ger* Rechten,
Belauert Perseus *bang* in seinem Schild
Der *schlummernden* Meduse Spiegelbild,
Das *süsse* Haupt mit *müden* Schlangenflechten.
Zur Hälfte zeigt der Spiegel längs der Erde
Des *jungen* Wuchses *atmende* Gebärde ...
"Raub' ich das *arge* Haupt mit *raschem* Hiebe.
Verderblich der Verderberin genaht?
Wenn nur die *blonde* Wimper schlummern bliebe!
Der Blick versteint! *Gefährlich* ist die That.
Die Mörderin! Sie schliesst vielleicht aus List
Die *wachen* Augen! Sie, die *grausam* ist!
Durch *weisse* Lider schimmert *blaues* Licht
Und — zischte dort der Kopf der Natter nicht?"[4]

MICHELANGELO UND SEINE STATUEN

Du *öffnest*, Sklave, deinen Mund,
Doch *stöhnst* du nicht.   Die Lippe *schweigt*,
Nicht *drückt*, Gedankenvoller, dich
Die Bürde der behelmten Stirn.
Du *packst* mit nerv'ger Hand den Bart,
Doch *springst* du, Moses, nicht empor.
Maria mit dem toten Sohn,
Du *weinst*, doch *rinnt* die Thräne nicht.
Ihr *stellt* des Leids Gebärde dar,
Ihr meine Kinder, ohne Leid!
So *sieht* der freigewordne Geist
Des Lebens überwundne Qual.
Was *martert* die lebend'ge Brust,
Beseligt und *ergötzt* im Stein.
Den Augenblick *verewigt* ihr,
Und *sterbt* ihr, *sterbt* ihr ohne Tod.
Im Schilfe *wartet* Charon mein,
Der *pfeifend* sich die Zeit *vertreibt*.[1]

In these sonorous, rhetorical poems, which combine sound and sense, one observes the solemn nobility, the aristocratic elegance, the majestic grandeur, the *maniera grande* at which Meyer aimed, and which he attained, in part, as we have been at pains to show, by his careful choice of words.

Gottfried Keller, to be sure, not appreciating the grand manner of his fastidious contemporary, refers to Meyer's hyper-refined style a trifle contemptuously as "brocade," and confides to a friend, ". . . dann gibt er sich zu sehr einem leisen Hang zur Manieriertheit, wo nicht Affektation des Stiles hin, was ich ihm einmal getreulich sagen werde,"[2] and writes to Storm, "Sobald ich am Menschen dieses unnötige Wesen und Sich-mausigmachen bemerke, so lasse ich ihn laufen."[1] In these remarks Keller may be said to have hit as a matter of fact upon one of the chief defects of Meyer's art, which is so full of mannerisms and affectation that it appears grand rather than great. With its insistence on nobility, sublimity, luxuriant grandeur, manifest in the repeated occurrence of epithets like *edel*,[2] *erhaben*,[3] *üppig*,[4] his *Poesie* is *Kunstpoesie*, his *Kunst*, *Luxuskunst*.[5] He is never, in Carl Busse's phrase, a poet of *Alltag* like Fontane, but instead the poet of *Festtag*, always "ein Talardichter," "un poète à toge."[6] "Ein goldner Helm von wundervoller Arbeit" is Liliencron's appreciative comment on Meyer's work,[7] but however true the characterization, one is tempted with d'Harcourt[8] to turn against Meyer the reproach which his own Hutten makes to the indifferent Erasmus, "Du bietest Gold und wir bedürfen Brod."

Meyer's careful selection of his vocabulary, his almost fastidious choice of words, are important factors, as we have heretofore observed, in the attainment of nobility of expression in his poetry and prose. Another noteworthy element in realizing his desire for the sublime grandeur which he summarized as the grand style and manner, is the terseness and concision, the compactness of his style. So laconic he is that Vischer called him in a letter "Tacitus der Novelle."[9] Kalischer cites Meyer as an example of

Feuerbach's definition, "Mit einem Wort: Stil ist richtiges Weglassen des Unwesentlichen."[1] Korrodi finds that "Meyers Kunst ist die Erfüllung des Schillerwortes geworden. Der Grosse Stil liegt nur in Wegwerfung des Zufälligen und in dem reinen Ausdruck des Notwendigen."[2] Linden concludes, "'Die Bildhauerei ist die Kunst des Wegnehmens,' sagt Michelangelo bei Varchi, und Meyer folgt ihm, mehr und mehr, bis zur äussersten Grenze der Manier, die nur in kurzen, erregten Sätzen redet."[3] Meyer himself expressed dislike, a veritable hatred, for "die Breite, die sogenannte 'Fülle.'"[4]

Meyer is like his Waser, "einer, der seine Worte wägt und keines zuviel sagen will";[5] like his Ludwig XIV, who asks "in seiner sachlichen Art, die kurze Wege liebte."[6] Like the Pfarrer of *Der Schuss von der Kanzel*, he is always condensing, giving much in little. "'Mein Amt, meine Würde!' wiederholte der Pfarrer langsam und schmerzlich. . . . Mit diesen vier schlichten Worten war dasselbe ausgedrückt, was uns in jener grossartigen Tirade erschüttert, mit welcher Othello von seiner Vergangenheit und seinem Amte Abschied nimmt."[7] "Mein Amt, meine Würde" is sufficient for Meyer. *Bene intelligenti pauca* seems his motto, as if he bore emblazoned on his banner the device which his heroine Gust Leubelfing chooses for herself, *Courte et bonne*.[8]

Meyer's condensation is the result of painstaking care and much labor. Contemplation of the various

metamorphoses of his poems and prose stories con-
vinces one of Meyer's "unermüdliches Streben, der
Form Adel und Prägnanz zu geben,"[1] and encourages
comment on his attempts to compress his statements
into ever shorter form.[2] Some phases of this compression, manifest in superficial matters like ellipses and
elisions, omissions of the article, and of the auxiliary
verb, I have elsewhere enumerated.[3] He seems to prefer simple tenses to compound, frequently employing
the preterite for the perfect, the past subjunctive for
the conditional.[4] We have seen him omitting the
noun, dignifying the adjective and participle as substantives.[5] The use of the past participle avoids a
dependent clause: "nach *gesungener* Hymne,"[6] "nach
erbrochenen Kisten und Kasten," [7] "die *weggeschleuderte* Kutte des Mönchs . . . die *vereinigten* Hände
Dianes und Astorres."[8] Here belong also Meyer's
frequent plays on words,[9] his fondness for concise
formulation of proverbs or sententious statements,
which give much in little.[10] One word with him often
does service for two: "So drehte er den Schnurrbart
und Ascanio das Steuerruder des Gesprächs";[11]
"Dann raffte er sich selbst und die Falten seines Purpurs zusammen"; [12] "Guicciardin zerdrückte den
feinen Kelch in der Hand und einen Fluch zwischen
den Zähnen";[13] "Er erschien wieder nach wenigen
Minuten und einer entsetzlichen That."[14]

There are plenty of examples of compact sum-
maries. Hutten, for example, sums up his impression

of Rome, "Sag' ich es kurz und klassisch, was ich sah /
Am Tiberstrom? Cloaca Maxima!"[1] Thespesius
recounts the story of his life:

> Hör' an! Ein Jüngling, peitscht' ich rasend das Ge-
> spann.
> Die Rosse flogen. Becher, Buhlen, Würfelspiel,
> Wut, Zorn, vergossen Blut — verklagend Blut!
> Dem ich entfloh, die Eumeniden hinter mir.[2]

Even the dash in the third line is an important descriptive device. The whole Calvinistic doctrine is
summarized in a single short stanza of the *Hugenotten-
lied*:

> In die Schule bin ich gangen
> Bei dem Meister Hans Calvin,
> Lehre hab' ich dort empfangen:
> Vorbestimmt ist alles ewighin!
> Jeder volle Wurf im Würfelspiele,
> Jeder Diebestritt auf Liebchens Diele,
> Jeder Kuss —
> Schicksalsschluss![3]

Like the Saracen heroine of his ballad *Mit zwei
Worten*, who with only two words, "London" and
"Gilbert," finds the way from Palestine to her lover
in England, as if to prove the assertion "Liebe wan-
dert mit zwei Worten gläubig über Meer und Land,"
Meyer with only two words, *Meer* and *Himmel*, describes her long trip:

> Sie betrat das Deck des Seglers, und ihr wurde nicht
> gewehrt.
> Meer und Himmel. "London?" frug sie, von der Heimat
> abgekehrt.[4]

He is extremely fond of such isolated nouns. In his prose one finds, for example, "Man verstand aus dem Dunkel: 'Jetzt schlummert der Mönch Astorre neben seiner Gattin Antiope.' *Und ein fernes Gelächter*";[1] or the phrase "*Und ein faunischer Jubel*"[2] standing as a complete sentence; or a new paragraph beginning "*Eine peinliche Pause*,"[3] as if to indicate a stage-setting, or to fill in the background of the scene. "Da näherte sich Astorre, das Knie gebogen, hob die Hände mit sich einander berührenden Fingerspitzen und seine bangen Blicke befragten das zarte Haupt auf dem blassen Goldgrunde. 'Findet Liebe Worte?' stammelte er. *Dämmerung und Schweigen*."[4]

Often a noun begins a poem, giving the setting much in the manner of a stage direction: "*Waldnacht. Urmächt'ge Eichen unter die . . .*";[5] "*Morgengrauen. Die Karawane . . .*";[6] "*Mondnacht und Flut. Sie hangt am Kiel*";[7] "*Ein leuchtend blauer Tag. Ein wogend Ährenfeld*, Daraus ein wetter-schwarzer. . . .*"[8]

These isolated nouns, often used almost like interjections, are dramatic descriptive agents:

Sie lösen ihre Stücke. *Rauch und Dampf.*
Es lichtet sich. *Standarten, Rossgestampf.*[9]

Es rauscht. Es raschelt. *Schritte* durch den Wald![10]

Vertreibt den Kauz vom Nest! Umarmt die Dirne! . . .
Geklirr! Ein Stein! . . . Still blutet eine Stirne.[11]

Horch! *Stimmen* durch den Wald! Ein *Lustgeschrei*!
Gekreisch! Gewieher! Freches Volk, vorbei![12]

Sometimes Meyer hurls a whole series of nouns at the reader in such rapid succession that they seem to pursue one another across the page:

Schande!   Brandmal!   Striemen!   Sklavenjoch!
Wehe!   Sie zerreissen dir das Kleid! [1]

Erstaunen!   Jubel!   Hohngelächter!   Spott!
Soldatenwitz: "Verendet hat der Gott!" [2]

Here we must learn to read not merely between lines but between words, for there is as much between the words as in them, as much suggested as explicitly expressed. Such a series of separate words was presumably in the mind of the critic who wrote, "Manchmal ist mir's bei C. F. Meyer, als ob er brennende Eisblocke dichtet. So stark ist die aufgespeicherte Spannung und der Luftdruck, unter dem der harte Kristall aufzulodern scheint." [3] Meyer's stanzas are surely surcharged; his poems, pregnant with meaning, are concentrated, condensed into solids at high temperature and pressure. The ordinary conventional *Backfischlyrik* [4] dilutes such a series of crystallized words into volumes of thin, watery *Gefühlsduselei*; Meyer, on the other hand, was always careful to boil down such weak solution to the very essence so that it should yield a precipitate. An early stanza of *Romanzen und Bilder*, for example, reads:

Roma Königin, wann endet doch
Über dir, der Götter Strafgericht?
Immer tiefer, immer tiefer noch

Neigst du dein geschändet Angesicht;
Denn Schmach und Klage
Wächst mit jedem Tage . . .
Sterben aber, Roma, kannst du nicht.[1]

Meyer's later condensation and concentration of these lines so energizes them that they are actually able to startle the reader:

Schande! Brandmal! Striemen! Sklavenjoch!
Wehe! Sie zerreissen dir das Kleid!
Ach wie lange noch, wie lange noch?
Stürbest, Göttin Roma, stürbst du doch!
Aber du bist voll Unsterblichkeit! [2]

All the later versions of his poems are highly elliptical as contrasted with the earlier versions. In the last stanza of *Der trunkene Gott*, a poem ten lines in length, which has only one adjective used as epithet and only two finite verbs, nouns in exclamation and participles used as adjectives and substantives combine to give concise brevity and rapid, dramatic movement:

Eine zürnende Gebärde!
Blitz und Sturz! Ein Gott in Wut!
Ein Erdolchter an der Erde
Windet sich in seinem Blut . . .
In den Abendlüften Schauer,
Ein verhülltes Haupt in Trauer,
Ausgerast und ausgegrollt!
Marmorgleich versteinte Zecher,
Und ein herrenloser Becher,
Der hinab die Stufen rollt.[3]

His prose also illustrates this appreciation of the statuesque solidity of the noun: "Ein tückischer

Becher ungewohnten *Weines*, oder das freche *Bild* einer ausschweifenden *Fabel*, oder der heisse *Hauch* des *Föhnes* . . . hatte ihn bethört und verstört. Und was er an den *Felsen* geschleudert, war nicht die *Schwester* . . . sondern irgend ein *Blendwerk* der *Gewitternacht*."[1] No less the graphic value of verbs: "Er *stiess* einen Schrei aus, *ergriff, schleuderte* sie, *sah* sie im Gewitterlicht gegen den Felsen *fahren, taumeln, tasten* und ihre Kniee unter ihr *weichen.* Er *neigte* sich über die *Zusammengesunkene*."[2]

His language seems sometimes preëminently the language of verbs:

Er *betrachtet* sein Kind.　Er *erstaunt.*　Er *erblasst.*
Er *entspringt* von entsetzlichem Grauen *erfasst.*
Er *flieht* im Gefild . . .[3]

The poem *Das Heiligtum* is an admirable illustration of this fondness for verbs:

Die heil'gen Eichen *drohen* Baum an Baum,
Die Römer *lauschen* bang und *atmen* kaum,
Schwer, schwerer wird der Hand des Beiles Wucht,
Und ihr *entsinkt*'s.　Sie *stürzen* auf die Flucht.
"*Steht!*" und sie *stehn.*　Denn es ist Cäsars Ruf,
Der ihre Seelen sich zu Willen *schuf!*
Er ist bei seiner Schar.　Er *deutet* hin
Auf eine Eiche.　Sie *umschlingen* ihn,
Sie *decken* ihn wie im Gedräng der Schlacht,
Sie *flehn.*　Er *ringt.*　Er hat sich *losgemacht,*
Er *schreitet* vor.　Sie *folgen.*　Er *ergreift*
Ein Beil, *hebt*'s, *führt* den Schlag, der *saust* und *pfeift*. . .
Sank er verwundet von dem frevlen Beil?
Er *lächelt*: "*Schauet*, Kinder, ich bin heil!"

nobility of expression and conciseness in his style, already discussed, there is manifest remarkable precision and plasticity. Fastidious in his choice of words, aspiring to nobility, terse in his selection, striving for compression, Meyer must be careful to choose the best possible word to achieve a maximum of effect by a minimum of means. To exploit each word to the utmost, he must be precise.

The revisions which Meyer undertakes in the verbs in his verses reveal this striving for greater precision, for a pregnancy of expression, which results not only in compact, compressed style but springs the imagination, in Meredith's phrase, to produce a clear-cut picture.[1] For the verb *senkt*,[2] originally used in the final lines of the poem *Der Marmorknabe*, Meyer substitutes *löscht*, so that the verse reads, "Er *löscht* die Fackel. Sie verloht. / Dieser schöne Jüngling ist der Tod,"[3] making it impossible to let life triumph by raising anew the torch which has now been really extinguished by death.[4] The eye of a black horse, *Der Rappe des Komturs*, turns to earth, not "als *säh*'," but "als *sucht*' es dort den toten Herrn. . . ."[5] "Wenn er isst und trinkt" becomes in Meyer, "*Wann* der *Kahle schwelgt* am *Mahl*,"[6] each word of which is characteristic, the poetical *wann* and *Mahl*, the specific verb *schwelgt*, the substantive adjective *der Kahle*, descriptive, picturesque, and precise, instead of the colorless personal pronoun or empty proper name. If Death appears, it is not enough to have him sit or stand; instead, "Im Stubenwinkel *grinst* der Tod."[1] Compression and precision are combined in the pregnant verb: "Ein reizend stumpfes Näschen *geckt* unter strupp'gem Schopf, / Mit wildem Mosesbart *prahlt* ein Charakterkopf."[2] The general gives way to the specific:

> Eine *gafft*
> Lüstern, eine *sinnt* dämonenhaft,
> Eine *lauscht* mit hartem Mördersinn.[3]

Realizing how little profit is to be derived from such verbs as are merely descriptive of position or condition, however precise, Meyer shows decided preference for verbs of motion, verbs of action. Instead of writing, "Der König *sagte*: 'Morgen will ich euch wieder *sehen*,'" or "*beobachten*," Meyer substitutes a more precise and active verb for these last two terms, namely *bestaunen*, and dispenses with the colorless, unnecessary *sagen* altogether, substituting for it a vigorous verb of action: "Der König *klatschte*: 'Morgen will / Ich wieder euch *bestaunen*.'"[4] The statement of a character is not merely quoted with a lame *sagt*, but accompanied by a gesture: "'Rom ist morgen euer!' *zeigt* Sever."[5] The comparatively mild lines,

> Nun tröstet mich das Eine doch
> Das päpstlich Joch
> *Es ist und bleibt zerschlagen*,[6]

become more vigorous in the final version, which is made to read,

Nun tröstet mich das Eine doch
Das päpstlich Joch
Ist in den Dreck getreten.[1]

It is not enough that an ill woman lie on her sick-bed; she tosses about: "Auf mondenhellem Lager *wälzt* ein Weib."[2]

The same principle is manifest, finally, in the changes which Meyer made in the last stanzas of *Hutten.* To a friend seeking to restrain him from jumping into the boat of the unknown ferryman Death, Meyer's hero Hutten voices objection:

Gib frei! Gib frei! Zurück! Ich spring' ins Boot. . . .
Fährmann . . . *wer bist du?* . . . Sprich! Bist du . . .
der Tod?

In the next version the uncertainty of the question to the ferryman Death is turned into definite recognition: "Fährmann, *ich kenne dich!* Du bist . . . der Tod." But this is not enough; the Hutten of the final version not only recognizes but greets Death: "Fährmann, *ich grüsse dich!* Du bist . . . der Tod!"[3]

Some of the many substitutions for the ordinary verb for walking, *gehen,* among which we enumerated, for example, *irren, pilgern, schleichen, schreiten, wallen, wandeln, wandern,* were doubtless selected merely to give nobility of expression to the style. Some, however, designate a certain kind of walking, a tendency to precision more clearly marked in the following examples: "*Hergestelzt* bin ich nach Flandern";[1] "Ihr selber *wankt* wie Schatten";[2] "Ein Weiblein *hinkt* mit Holz vorbei."[3]

Being so precise in his choice of verbs and always careful to exploit every opportunity to give much in little, Meyer rarely introduces dialogue with the ordinary verb *sagen*. It is too general and colorless, not specific or precise enough. He spurns a mere *inquit*, therefore, substituting for the ordinary form *said* a whole variety of verbs: answered, asked, began, begged, confessed, continued, cried, ejaculated, ended, explained, implored, laughed, moaned, ordered, rejoiced, remarked, replied, roared, thundered, wailed, whispered, and so on. Not content with these, he becomes still more precise. It is not enough to substitute *lachte er* for *sagte er*. Meyer must at least write *hohnlachte er*, indicating a special kind of laughter in derision. So *lächelte* becomes *hohnlächelte* or *grinste* or *kicherte*. The ordinary *whispered* is capable of several variations: *flüsterte, hauchte, lallte, lispelte, murmelte, stammelte, stotterte, wisperte*. Not enough to have *spottete*, we must have *spöttelte* or such rare substitutes for *sagte* as *giftelte, stichelte*. We find *deklamierte, docirte, examinierte, parodierte, philosophierte*, and the whole scale of different moods and intonations expressed by *ächzte, bleckte, brummte, girrte, heulte, keuchte, kicherte, krächzte, krähte, kreischte, näselte, schluchzte, schnarrte, stöhnte, wimmerte, zischte*. In his poems we find: "'Dieser!' *höhnt* es im Gedränge, / 'Dieser Trotz'ge!' *zischt* die Menge";[4]

"Die Dunkle *höhnt*";[1] "Die Lichte *fleht*";[2] "Der Schreckensbleiche *stammelt*";[3] and in his prose in four pages in rapid succession: "*lallte* er," "*seufzte* der Mönch," "*zürnte* er," "*raste* der Alte," "*raunte* der Tyrann," "*mahnte* Ezzelin," "*schluchzte* der Mönch," "*fragte* ein Priester," "*rief* der Sterbende," "*schrie* der Mönch," "*frohlockte* er," "*drängte* der Alte," "*murmelte* der Sterbende."[4] Without burdening ourselves with an enumeration of the more than two hundred and fifty of such single substitutions for *sagte* which Meyer has at his command, exclusive of the substitutions of a whole phrase which he sometimes employs,[5] we may conclude from the examples cited that he makes the most, almost too much, of comparatively modest opportunities for description.

A similar extreme love of explicit verbs and an exaggerated desire for precision makes the same Meyer, whom we have heretofore discovered extraordinarily chary of words, become, on occasion, extravagant and almost lavish.[6] In his poems we read: "Jede Stufe *strotzt* und *wogt* und *schwillt*";[7] "Eine Rede *schwirrt* und *irrt* und *rauscht*";[8] "So *rieselt* sanft und *wächst* und *schwillt*";[9] "Jeder First, der *raucht* und *dampft* und *lodert*";[10] "Es *reizt*, es *quält*, es *schlüpft*, es *schmiegt* / Sich zwischen Edelknecht und Maid";[11] "Nicht was sich *dreht* und *schwingt* und *spritzt* und *sprüht*";[12] "Im Korne drunten *wogt* und *weht* / Und *rauscht* und *wühlt* der Föhn."[13] Similarly, in his prose: "Es *redete*, es *rief*, es

dröhnte";[1] "*Frage, untersuche, prüfe*";[2] "Aber dann
kommt der Witz und *klügelt* und *lächelt* und *redet* uns
die Gefahr aus";[3] "Ein Nachbar *streckt* den Kopf
durch die Thürspalte, *predigt, straft, mischt* sich ein";[4]
"Jetzt erhob sich drunten auf dem Platze ein *Murren*,
ein *Schelten*, ein *Verwünschen*, ein *Drohen*";[5] "*Weh-
klagend, scheltend, drohend, beschwörend* warf sich ihr
die Aebtissin mit ihren Nonnen in den Weg";[6] "So
rief und *flehte* sie und *küsste* und *herzte* und *drückte* den
Pagen";[7] "Das niederste und schlimmste Volk—
*Beutelschneider, Kuppler, Dirnen, Betteljungen—blies,
kratzte, paukte, pfiff, quiekte, meckerte* und *grunzte*
vor und hinter einem abenteuerlichen Paare."[8]
The collective noun *Volk*, even though qualified by
two extremely limiting adjectives, is too inclusive; it
must be resolved into its component parts; a general
verb implying noise would seem lacking in dramatic
vigor, the specific acts must stand out, the reader's
attention be focused in turn on no less than seven different actions.

The exact action, the exact actor must be specified
by Meyer, who is no less precise in his verbs than in
his nouns: "Zu Wald! Zu Wald! Der Rappe *scharrt*! /
Die Bracke *spürt*!   Die Rüde *bleckt*! / Ein Geier
krächzt in seinem Horst, / In heller Lichtung *äst* ein
Hirsch."[9] In verbs like *scharrt, spürt, bleckt, äst*,
Meyer singles out specific, characteristic acts, just as
he prefers *Rappe* to *Pferd* and makes the general noun
Hund more specific in *Bracke* and *Rüde*.

We have found Meyer before preferring to the ordinary term *Pferd* the more elevated terms *Ross, Gaul, Renner.*[1] Like *Pferd*, these are generic terms, however, too inclusive for Meyer, who substitutes the species for the genus, the specific for the general. A *Pferd* in Meyer does not remain a *Pferd*, but becomes a *Hengst*[2] or a *Stute*,[3] depending on its sex; an *Araber*,[4] a *Berber*,[5] an *andalusiches Vollblut*,[6] depending on its blood. Sex, blood, also color, must be designated either by an adjective or more commonly by the noun itself: "auf *einem schneeweissen Zelter*";[7] "*ein Falber*";[8] "*ein Brauner*";[9] "*ein Fuchs*";[10] "*ein Rappe*";[11] "*ein Schimmel.*"[12] The designation becomes even more exact; the horse must be "*ein falber Berber*"[13] or "*ein arabischer Grauschimmel*": "*Voran der Kanzler, den ich an seinem wunderschlanken, arabischen Grauschimmel* erkannte."[14] For one can really recognize the heroes of Meyer by their horses, carefully selected to be in keeping with their character. Thomas Becket is regularly mounted on a white Arabian mare;[15] Jürg Jenatsch is recognized by his fiery, restless black charger,[16] his *Rappe*, which remains also the favorite mount of Pescara, as the *Fuchs* is of Herzog Rohan.

Meyer finds a horse a more colorful means of characterizing a hero than a mere name. Only rarely is he content to refer to a character by his name or a personal pronoun. Realizing the validity of Juliet's plea to Romeo, he finds that there is little in a name that can serve as a characteristic or sensuous description and still less in a colorless personal pronoun which is the same for all men and all time. Intent as always on making much of little and exploiting every possibility to the full, Meyer prefers to the proper name or the personal pronoun designations which shall reveal something of the man, his origin, his connections, perhaps some of his physical, mental, or moral qualities. Thus in *Die Hochzeit des Mönchs* Dante is referred to as *"der Florentiner,"*[1] Herr Burcardo as *"der Alsatier"*;[2] in *Pescara*, Guicciardin is *"der Florentiner,"*[3] Lälius *"der Venezianer."*[4] Ascanio in the first of these two stories is not simply *Ascanio* or *er*; instead, he is variously referred to as *"der Neffe"*[5] of Ezzelin or *"der Günstling Ezzelins"*[6] or *"der Heitere,"*[7] *"der Achtlose,"*[8] *"der Verzückte,"*[9] *"der Muthige,"*[10] as, in the same story, Ezzelin is commonly *"Der Grausame,"*[11] and a woman character *"Die Empfindsame."*[12] Germano the warrior becomes *"Der Gepanzerte"*[13] or, on one special occasion, *"Der Ungepanzerte,"*[14] as Wulfrin in *Die Richterin* is regularly *"Der Behelmte,"*[15] another character *"Der Benarbte."*[16] On the same page on which Germano is *"Der Gepanzerte,"* he is also *"der Schnurrbärtige,"*[17] for he is the man "der einen Ringelpanzer und einen lang herabhangenden Schnurrbart trug,"[18] as Meyer concisely describes him. So other characters are not mentioned by name but appear as *"der Bärtige,"*[19] or still more exactly as *"der Weissbart,"*[20] *"der Grau-*

bart,"[1] *"der Rothbart."*[2] Not even the minor characters are left shadowy and indistinct. An unnamed character, speaking on occasion, is not simply *einer*, but etched out as *"der Rothbart,"*[3] to be referred to a page later as *"der Lange."* Thus in a description of a mob scene: *"Ein hagerer Mensch* liess seine mythologischen Kenntnisse glänzen." Mentioned again, he is called *"die Hopfenstange"*; introduced a third time, overtaken by misfortune, he is *"der Elende."*[4] The duke in *Angela Borgia*, returning from Rome, dismounting from his horse, and stained with travel, is not simply the duke, *der Herzog*, but *"der Staubbedeckte"*: "Die Diener, welche ihm die Thür öffneten wegdrängend, trat der Herzog ein. 'Ich komme von Rom,' begann *der Staubbedeckte."*[5] In *Das Leiden eines Knaben* names are at times dispensed with altogether. One speaker in the heated dialogue is simply *"Der Wolf,"* another — *horribile dictu!* — *"der Nasige"*:

"Mentiris impudenter!" heulte *der Wolf*.

"Mentiris impudentissime, pater reverende!" überschrie ihn *der Nasige*, an allen Gliedern zitternd.[6]

A common substitute for a proper name or for a personal pronoun in Meyer's stories is a descriptive adjective used substantively, a device by which Meyer gains, as we have observed before,[7] both nobility and compression of style. Substituting for a nondescript proper name or drab and dreary pronoun

a substantive adjective which gives a physical attribute or a mental state of his character, using different
adjectives for the same character, selecting always the
one best suited to his purpose, Meyer attains considerable descriptive precision. Ascanio is *"der Heitere,"*
"der Achtlose," "der Muthige": *"Der Muthige* begann zu zittern."[1] Gasparde, once referred to as *"die
Schlanke,"*[2] is, when more fitting, *"die Bleiche"*:
"Ich hatte Gasparde auf mein Lager gebettet, wo *die
Bleiche* zu schlummern schien."[3] Like the Lucrezia
Borgia of his story, — "Von jetzt an nannte Lucrezia
den Dämon, der ihr Bruder gewesen war, nicht anders
mehr als *den Aermsten,* so wie sie ihr Ungeheuer von
Vater längst *den Guten* nannte,"[4] — Meyer uses descriptive adjectives substantively to help characterize
his personages: *"Die Dunkle* höhnt";[5] *"Die Lichte*
fleht";[6] *"Der Schreckensbleiche* stammelt";[7] in these
phrases the adjectives are no less precise than the
verbs. Elsewhere in his verses he has characters appearing to whom he refers as *"die Bange,"*[8] *"die
Blonde,"*[9] *"die Bleiche,"*[10] *"der Kahle,"*[11] *"der
Kühne,"*[12] *"der Schreckliche,"*[13] *"die Zarte,"*[14] and so
on. "'Wie anders, Herrin,' fieberte *die Unselige* . . .
'aber du treibst dein Spiel mit mir, *Grausame.'"*[15] The
same device is elsewhere very frequently employed.[16]

When Meyer writes, "Lasst den Mönch reden, dass
wir teilnehmend erfahren, wie er sich abwendete von
einer *Rohen* zu einer *Zarten,* einer *Kalten* zu einer
Fühlenden, von einem steinernen zu einem schlagen-

den Herzen,"[1] he manifests fondness for the participle used substantively as well as for the adjective.
The substitution of the substantive participle for a
proper name has as a matter of fact all the merits of
the adjective so used, in lending compression, nobility
and grandeur to style and in not merely giving a
physical quality or mental state of the person designated but revealing him in action: "Dem *Verfemten*
folgte sie, dem *Flieh'nden*, / Durch die Schluchten
des Gebirges *Zieh'nden. . . .*"[2] Characters are frequently referred to as "die *Schwankende*,"[3] "die
Gequälte,"[4] "die *Spähende*,"[5] "der *Rasende*,"[6] "die
in *Ungnade Gerathene* aber nun genug *Geprüfte*."[7]
The Kanzler is "der sonst nach allen Seiten *Um-
blickende* und das Keimen der Dinge *Belauschende*";[8]
Diana is "die *Gekränkte* und ihr Recht *Fordernde*,
die *Gedrückte*, die immer *Geopferte*."[9] We grow accustomed to reading, "Dieser betrachtete die *sich
umschlungen Haltenden*";[10] "Wird sich eine *Be-
schämte* und *Geschlagene* einem Ritter verweigern";[11]
"Warum zerrtest du nicht einen *Taumelnden* aus den
Armen einer *Berauschten*?"[12]

The same practice of substituting the definite for
the indefinite, the specific for the general, a concrete
and graphic term for one that is abstract and barren,
is no less clearly manifest in Meyer's selection of adjectives than in his choice of verbs and nouns. Instead of heaping epithet on epithet, which the sur-
feited reader might find difficult to assimilate, Meyer,

not unlike Grillparzer,[1] appears to follow Lessing's principle: "Ebenso kann auch die Poesie in ihren fortschreitenden Nachahmungen nur eine einzige Eigenschaft des Körpers nutzen und muss daher diejenige wählen, welche das sinnlichste Bild des Körpers ... erweckt."[2] He endeavors to focus attention on one characteristic feature, the *punctum saliens*. In this manner his poems picture nature:

> Er schwingt es weit, er mäht und mäht
> Und Etzels Schwert, es schwelgt und trinkt,
> Bis müd die Sonne niedergeht
> Und hinter *rote* Wolken sinkt;[3]

and portray people:

> Unsichtbarem Geisselhiebe
> Beugt sie sich in Qual und Liebe,
> Auf den *zarten* Knieen liegend,
> Enge sich zusammenschmiegend;[4] —

"Hart an die Scheibe presst' das *junge* Weib / Die *bleiche* Stirn";[5] "Auf einem *blanken* Kissen schlummernd liegt / Ein *feiner* Mädchenkopf."[6] The cardinal of *Angela Borgia* is represented as "die *hagere* Gestalt in Purpur";[7] the feature emphasized in Thomas Becket is "sein *bleiches* Haupt,"[8] in Pescara "das *mächtige* Antlitz."[9]

By emphasis of one trait at a time, the characters are described not only in unobtrusive fashion, but in a manner which makes imaginal assimilation of the elements in the description fairly simple. Sforza of

Die Versuchung des Pescara is introduced on page 1
as "der *junge* Herzog Sforza," with mere mention of
"die *melancholischen* Augen." Page 2 adds "auf dem
feinen Munde des Herzogs," "seinen *binsenschlanken*
Körper"; page 3 "die *spitzen* Kniee"; page 4 "seine
magere Wange." Thus the small figure of this young
duke, whom Morone continually addresses affection-
ately as "Fränzchen," gradually becomes a familiar
figure to the reader. Similarly the elements in the
personality of Jürg Jenatsch are singly presented. On
his first appearance we read simply, "und drückte
mit dem Rufe 'Herzenswaser!' den Freund an seine
breite Brust";[1] but his physical and moral qualities
soon follow, one at a time: "der *athletische* Mann,"[2]
"eine *hohe* Gestalt,"[3] "der *teuflische* Jenatsch,"[4]
"eine *grosse* Gestalt,"[5] "von *gewaltiger* Statur,"[6] "von
herrischem Blick,"[7] "das *feurige* Gesicht,"[8] "die
trotzige Haltung,"[9] "von *gewaltigem* Wuchs,"[10] "sein
feuriges Antlitz."[11]   Selecting one trait at a time,
Meyer concentrates attention on that: "eine *grosse*
Gestalt"; "ein Kriegsmann von *gewaltiger* Statur und
herrischem Blick";[12] "die *hohe* Gestalt und die *trotzige* Haltung des Jürg Jenatsch."[13] This tall, powerful figure with defiant, diabolic countenance, from
whose hat wave plumes of blue, who is clad in a
cloak of flaming scarlet and mounted on his fiery,
restive steed, which stamps and roars and champs its
bit, flecking its shiny black coat with spatters of
white foam — this superb figure seems firmly chis-

elled out and stands distinct before us in sharp visual outline, as if in glorious illustration and conclusive proof of Meyer's ability, "plastisch greifbare Gestalten hervorzuzaubern und sie handelnd auftreten zu lassen": "Und da war er! Auf seinem schäumenden Rappen in der Mitte des leeren Raumes von Allen gemieden";[1] "Voran auf einem schwarzen Hengst ein Reiter in Scharlach, von dessen Stülphute blaue Federn wehten, der jedem Kinde bekannte Jürg Jenatsch."[2]

In the story to which this hero gives the title mention is made of a vague rumor, "Doch alles schwebte und schwankte in unbestimmten Umrissen,"[3] an unfamiliar condition in the stories of Meyer, who is always intent in his creative endeavors to achieve the contrary, rejoicing that under his revising hand a narrative has gained firm outlines, "an deutlichem Umriss gewonnen hat."[4] He resembles in this respect his character Papst Clemens, who in his interview with Victoria feels he must reveal all in full light and in clear outline: "die Sache in klaren Umrissen vorzeichnen und in ein volles Licht stellen."[5] Meyer found in Romance literatures the sharp contours and illuminated figures which much of misty German literature seemed to him to lack. In the very revelatory interview with Fritz Kögel he remarked, "In der deutschen Literatur empfinde ich einen Mangel: das ist nicht scharf genug gesehen, nicht sinnlich herausgestellt, es ist unbildlich verschwimmend. Die

Gleichnisse und Bilder im Deutschen sind schwach,
sie erhellen und beleuchten nicht. Dagegen die
Ariosts. . . ."[1] To Nanny Escher he recommends as
the best method of securing the most pregnant expression the translation of German phrases into French.[2]
That Meyer himself learned much from imitation of
French models is clear enough; his prose shows a precision and plasticity rare in German, which may well
have been derived from reading in French literature,[3]
for which Meyer confessed a pronounced stylistic
preference in his statement to Louise von François,
"Vergessen Sie nicht, dass ich 10 Jahre meines Lebens (25–35) französisch gewesen bin. So ist mir
eine Vorliebe geblieben — auch für die rein stilistischen Vorzüge der französischen Literatur."[4]

Our interest is less, however, in the probable Romance sources of Meyer's style than in his actual
stylistic accomplishment in German. The compression, precision, plasticity, which we have observed in
his selection of words, are admirably illustrated in the
compact titles to his poems and stories, with their
striving for precise and pregnant formulation and
their concern with carefully selected concrete objects
or persons. The specific and personal *Der Marmorknabe* replaces the more general and impersonal *Das
Marmorbild* as the title of a poem. *Der Gesang der
Parze*, which suggests that a fate is being spun, is preferred to the ambiguous and comparatively meaning-
less *Die Römerin* as the title of a second, just as the

more revealing *Die wunderbare Rede* takes the place of the empty *Das Amphitheater* as the title of a third.[1] The name of a person which Meyer does not find descriptive enough for use in the body of a story is rarely selected to do service as a title. A more expressive formula which will throw light on the character or give the motif of the work is substituted for the proper name of hero or heroine. *Margarita* becomes *Die Ketzerin*; the story dealing with her who sits in judgment is not called merely *Stemma* but *Die Richterin*. *Page Leubelfing* is rejected for the title which incorporates a more august personage whom the heroine serves, *Gustav Adolfs Page*. The story which was printed in the periodical *Deutsche Rundschau* as *Das Brigittchen von Trogen* appears in book form with the title *Plautus im Nonnenkloster*,[2] which puts two concrete objects in a very curious, almost contradictory, collocation, just as in two other surprising and somewhat enigmatic titles, *Der Schuss von der Kanzel* and *Die Hochzeit des Mönchs*.

Not only do these titles arouse the reader's interest by the hidden queries they contain: What is Plautus doing in a convent? When, why, and from whom comes a shot from the pulpit? When, why, and whom can a monk marry? But they, no less than the stories themselves, reveal the firm outlines of concrete, material objects. Poggio is correct in commencing his account of Plautus in the convent, "Meine Facetie . . . handelt von zwei Kreuzen, einem schweren und einem leichten."[1]   The two other stories are likewise built up on a confusion between two concrete objects, two pistols in the *Schuss*, two rings in the *Mönch*, just like two crosses in *Plautus*.   Like Heinrich von Kleist, who selects a concrete material object on which to hinge his plot and let discussion and action revolve, — the *Handschuh* of *Prinz Friedrich*, the *Rappen* of *Michael Kohlhaas*, the *Perücke* and the *Zerbrochene Krug* in his comedy of that title, — so Meyer chooses the pistols, rings, and crosses of these three stories, the *Axt* in *Jürg Jenatsch*, and *Das Amulett*, which is permitted to stand as the title of a story, as *Die Ampel* remains the title of a poem.[2]

Other poems bear the concrete titles *Der Blutstropfen* and *Stapfen* — definite, material forms whose outlines are so fixed and firm that they are used by authors of German metrical romances of the Middle Ages as graphic objects to conjure up an emotion or a loved figure, like the three drops of blood in the snow in Wolfram's *Parzival* and the telltale footsteps in Gottfried's *Tristan*.

In the poem *Stapfen*, Meyer, returning home alone after a walk with his loved one, as if in illustration of the phrase *ex pede Herculem*, reconstructs her very picture from the footprints in the road:

> Die Stapfen schritten jetzt entgegen dem
> Zurück dieselbe Strecke Wandernden:
> Aus deinen Stapfen hobst du dich empor
> Vor meinem innern Auge.[3]

Meyer, like Wordsworth, is able to conjure up images upon "the inward eye"; indeed he tells us so in his verses: "Mit den Augen meines Geistes / Schwelg' ich in den lichten Wundern."[1] He confides to one visitor, "Allmählich gewinnen die Gestalten meiner Forschung vor meinem geistigen Auge schärfere Formen, endlich leuchtende Farben und warmes pulsierendes Leben,"[2] and confesses to another his desire "alles nach aussen hin schaubar, sichtbar zu gestalten."[3] In view of the ability which his first biographer, Frey, finds in him, "Durch energische Vergegenwärtigung eines Vorganges, durch langes, wiederholtes Hinblicken darauf gelang es ihm, eine Scene plastisch, völlig bildmässig zu sehen und die entscheidenden Linien, Züge und Farben gleichsam abzulesen,"[4] German critics have called him an *Augenmensch* or *Eidetiker*; French, a *visuel*.[5] Certainly "die Fähigkeit des Plastisch- und Farbigsehens," which he confesses was not congenital with him, is highly developed in his writings.[6]

Instead of asking simply, "Was denkst du von Pescara?" Meyer's character, pointing him out in a portrait, inquires, "Was denkst du von dem hier mit dem *rothen Wamse*?"[7] substituting a picture for a proper name, realizing the truth of the old Chinese proverb that one picture is worth ten thousand words, illustrating what Meyer expressed to his sister Betsy, that a poet must not merely say things but show them.[8] It is as if the reader were continually ad-

monishing him in the words of Wagner's Siegfried:
"dir glaub' ich nicht mit dem Ohr, dir glaub' ich nur
mit dem Aug'," and demanding with Othello "the
ocular proof." After one takes monastic orders, one
is naturally enough "*ein Geschorener*";[1] in Meyer's
story the room occupied by Astorre before he became
a monk is referred to as "[dieselbe Thurmstube], die
Astorre als *Knabe mit ungeschorenen Locken* be-
wohnt."[2]   Concrete objects are substituted as symbols to represent abstract concepts in order to make a
demonstration *ad oculos*. Astorre's crime in renounc-
ing his vows and betraying his trust as both friar and
knight is phrased to read, "Darf Astorre leben?
Kann er es, jetzt da er nach verschleuderter Sandale
auch den angezogenen ritterlichen Schuh zur Schlarpe
tritt und der Cantus firmus des Mönches in einem
gellenden Gassenhauer vertönt?"[3]   Racine's bloodless, intellectual line, "Je voudrais, disait-il, ne savoir
pas écrire," becomes in Meyer's translation, "O
hätte nie die Hand gelernt den Stift zu führen,"[4] in
which two concrete objects, *Hand* and *Stift*, which
may be seen and felt, take the place of rationalistic
generalities.

Commenting on Schiller's poem *Das Ideal und das
Leben*, Meyer remarks to his sister, "Dieser in seiner
starken Geduld alles überwindende Herkules ist herr-
lich: 'Alle Plagen, alle Erdenlasten / Wälzt der un-
versöhnten Göttin List / Auf die will'gen Schultern
des Verhassten. . . .'   Welch ein Bild! Siehst du es

nicht vor dir: diese gebeugten, willigen Schultern?"[1] Whether Schiller saw these shoulders, or even meant them to be seen, is immaterial; the interesting part of the observation is that Meyer singles them out, as in his poetry he selects concrete objects, especially parts of the body, which seem the characteristic feature, and localizes interest there, letting the part stand for the whole. This is clearly apparent in various changes in the titles of his poems. *Lucia Vendogoli* becomes *Das Zeichen*, later *Die gezeichnete Stirn*; *Don Juan de Austria* becomes *Das Auge des Blinden*; *Der Hugenot* becomes *Die Füsse im Feuer*, so that we may have definite parts of the body before us: *Stirn*, *Auge*, *Füsse*.

In the poems and stories themselves we read, not "Da umschlang das Mädchen *Lucrezia*," but "Da umschlang das Mädchen die *Schultern* Lucrezias";[2] not "er keuchte" but "Seine *Brust* keuchte."[3] A deserting lover goes, not to another woman, but to another woman's breast, "Vielleicht den Herzgeliebten, welcher sie / An eines andern Weibes *Brust* verriet."[4] One does not cry vaguely for help or even for the help of some definite person; instead, "Wo ist die gepanzerte rettende *Hand*, dass ich sie ergreife?"[5] In an Alpine hut it is not the old woman who spins but "Einer Greisin welke *Hand*."[6] Of Dante we read, "Die *Hand*, welche heute Terzinen geschmiedet hat — diese wuchtige *Hand*."[7] It is not merely the miserliness of her parent that hinders Diana's marriage;

that is a colorless abstraction; the concrete obstacle is "die geschlossene *Hand* ihres Vaters."[1] The boy does not crush the glass: "Des Jungen *Faust* zerdrückt das Glas."[2] One does not deal with the emperor, the Spanish, the Swiss, but "mit den groben *Fäusten* der Schweizer, den langen *Fingern* des Kaisers, — und den spanischen Meuchler*händen*."[3] So one renders up jewels, not to the goldsmith, but "den gekrümmten *Fingern* des Goldschmieds."[4] "Then Mirabelle rapped" reads, "Dann klopfte der *Finger* Mirabellens."[5] Proceeding from hand to finger to fingertips, one finds that in Meyer one plays the lute "mit den *Fingerspitzen*";[6] "Miguel ist fort und wieder da, / Die *Fingerspitze* zeigend."[7] Even the unusual and almost over-precise word for the very top of the fingertip is called into service: "der einst aus ihrer *Fingerbeere* gespritzte Blutstropfen."[8]

We can proceed in Meyer's stories from hand to foot, from *Hand, Faust, Finger*, to *Fuss, Sohle, Ferse*. We do not observe a woman in haste, we focus our eye on her "eilenden *Füsse*."[9] A boy does not bleed; his feet drip blood: "Knabe, deine Blicke trauern! Jüngling, deine *Füsse* bluten."[10] A poem tells of the return, not of the mourners, but of their feet: "Als die *Füsse* derer wiederkehrten, / Die den Toten vor das Thor getragen."[11] "She burns with impatience" is not merely kept as a commonplace metaphor, localized in the heart; it is extended to the very soles of the feet: "Herz und *Sohlen* brannten ihr vor Ungeduld."[12] In

Meyer's fastidious phrase, one walks not "auf nackten Füssen" but "auf nackten *Sohlen*";[1] a horseman
rides "mit nackten *Fersen*."[2] Guests find it advisable
"bis auf die letzte *Ferse* zu verschwinden."[3] Astorre
walks down "eine mit Gras bewachsene verschattete
Gasse . . . die seinen *Sandalen* wohlbekannt war."[4]
Meyer's striving for precision makes him over-fastidi-
ous, hyper-refined, very mannered in these precious
synecdoches, which descend from *Finger* to *Fingerspitze*, from *Fuss* to "Eines allerliebsten *Fusses /
Weisses Spitzchen* in die Luft."[5]
Reversing the usual order of top to toe, we find
Meyer particularly fond of portraying heads, like the
sculptor of whom his Poggio tells: "Der alte Meister
hatte — absichtlich, oder wohl eher aus Mangel an
künstlerischen Mitteln — Körper und Gewandung
roh behandelt, sein Können und die Inbrunst seiner
Seele auf die Köpfe verwendend."[6] Not from any
lack of resources, but for a very definite artistic purpose Meyer does the same. "Drei *Köpfe* rückten
zusammen"[7] is a characteristic formulation. Gustav
Adolf, looking about in an assembly, sees "schlaue
neben verwegenen, ehrgeizige neben beschränkten,
fromme neben frechen *Köpfen*."[8] The head and face
are selected for inspection. Not enough to inspect
people, we really examine faces: "Dieser musterte die
anwesenden *Gesichter*."[9] We are dissatisfied with the
impression made upon us, not by people, but by
their faces: "Mit meiner *Miene* schien er nicht zufrie-

den."[1] Similarly Dante hears from a gracious auditor: "'Meine *Miene* gebe ich dir preis,' sagte grossartig die Fürstin."[2] One does not tremble before an innocent angel, but one may well quake "vor dem unschuldvollen *Engelsantlitz*."[3] Two people do not sing from the same book; instead, "Aus demselben Psalmenbuche / Sang das frische *Jugendantlitz* beider."[4] Not enough to long for people, one longs for faces and features: "und bin scharf geritten, da ich mich nach Euerm *Antlitz* sehnte, liebe Frau";[5] "mich verlangte nach dem *Antlitz* meines Wohlthäters";[6] or finally even the daring *pars pro toto*, "Hätte ich Flügel! mich verlangt nach den *Narben* meines Herrn."[7]

Meyer chooses for inspection not merely the head, the face, some especial feature — nay, some precise portion of that feature. The question which troubles memory is not "Wo sah ich dich?" but "Wo sah ich, Mädchen, deine *Züge*?"[8] In meeting an old acquaintance one does not cry on recognition, "Er ist's." Instead, on looking closer, Meyer's character finds "die unverschämte *Stumpfnase* und unter einem Juristenbarett das freche *Kraushaar*, das ich von Pavia her kenne."[9] One does not feel sympathy for a person; instead, "beschlich ihn noch ein Mitleid mit den guten braunen *Augen* und dem zahnlosen *Munde*."[10] One does not simply wash; instead, we watch "während er ihr *Stirn* und *Lid* und *Wange* wusch und badete,"[11] a resolving of the act into its various component parts, which helps to present a graphic picture. *Wange* is preferred as more precise than *Gesicht*; not the face burns, but "Des Meisters hohle *Wange* brennt."[1] One's face is not scratched with thorns, but one's cheek: "eine von Dornen zerkritzte *Wange*."[2] One does not sit head in hand, but chin in hand: "in der Hand barg er das *Kinn*";[3] or forehead in hand: "Die arbeitende *Stirn* in die Linke gelegt."[4] Insanity does not come over people; instead, "und der Wahn gewann Macht über diese *Stirn*."[5] Dante, looking around among his auditors, "entdeckte — neben mancher flachen einige bedeutende *Stirnen*."[6] The question is put to him: "Erzählst du uns eine wahre Geschichte, mein Dante, nach Dokumenten? oder eine Sage des Volksmundes? oder eine Erfindung deiner bekränzten *Stirne*?"[7] Meyer's fondness for localizing interest in concrete parts of the body, on *Stirne*,[8] leads him even to such usages as "Der Mund des Einen verzog sich in der Dämmerung zum Spott, während die *Stirne* des Andern sann und grübelte";[9] "Wärest du eine Böse, woher nähmest du das Recht und die *Stirn*, das Böse aufzudecken und zu richten,"[10] for the abstract word *Recht* must not go without a most concrete *Stirn*.

From *Stirn* we turn to *Wange*, from *Wange* to the *Nase*, which it frames. People do not nod, nor do their heads, but their noses do: "Die langen welschen *Nasen* nickten fein."[11] The observant young maiden who becomes *Gustav Adolfs Page* bursts into the room with the words: "Was hat's gegeben, Herr Ohm und

Herr Vetter? Ihr habt ja Beide ganz bleiche *Nasen-spitzen*!"[1]

More attention is directed to the mouth and lips: "'Thörinnen!' gellt ein scharfgeschnittner *Mund*";[2] "Du bist's! Doch deine *Lippen* schweigen";[3] "Du öffnest, Sklave, deinen *Mund*, / Doch stöhnst du nicht. Die *Lippe* schweigt";[4] "Ascanios muthwillige *Lippen* erstaunen";[5] "Die blassen *Lippen* schaudern vor dem Wein."[6] Meyer's King Henry longs not for a reconciliation with the chancellor in the abstract, nor for the figure of the chancellor himself, but to meet his lips in a forgiving kiss: "so heiss dürstete ihn nach der Berührung der *Lippen*, die seine langjährigen Qualen stillen und seinem Leben den Frieden geben sollten."[7] For the lips are among the important features for Meyer, to judge from the frequent occurrence of *Lippen*.[8] The corners of the mouth, which are such an important indication of mood, are also frequently mentioned. In a poem he writes, "Still in den *Winkeln des Mundes* lächelt ein grausamer Zug."[9] He closes the first chapter of *Pescara* with the sentence, "Dieser war bleich wie der Tod, mit einem Lächeln in den *Mundwinkeln*."[10] Even the palate is mentioned: "Da gab's keine Schenken / Für durstende *Gaumen* und siedendes Blut."[11] At least once the beard, which adorns so many of Meyer's heroes, becomes a symbol for the man: "Nun die hübsche Sünderin. Ich anvertraue sie deinem weissen *Barte*."[12]

Ears and eyes, *Ohr* and *Auge*, are frequently employed to localize attention. Morone is informed "durch die spähenden *Ohren*, welche er unter dem Gesinde Pescaras besoldete."[1] Another character at the court is characterized as an eye and ear: "Ist er doch an unserm Hofe das lauschende *Ohr*, das spähende *Auge*."[2] "Das spähende *Auge*" plays a very important rôle in Meyer's poems and stories, in his whole artistic production. The cardinal does not say to Don Giulio, "ich verbiete Dir, Angela anzusehen"; he commands, "ich verbiete Dir das *Antlitz* Angelas! Ich verbiete Dir ihre *Augen*!"[3] Similarly Pescara warns Don Juan: "Vermeidet heute die *Augen* Donna Victorias! Euer Antlitz ist ihnen verhasst, sie können einen Mörder nicht ertragen."[4] "Dante suchte den Sprecher" is phrased by Meyer to read, "Dantes *Auge* suchte den Sprecher."[5] "Du spottest" becomes "Deine *Augen* spotten, Prinz."[6] "Da freute sich Palma" becomes "Da freuten sich die *Augen* Palmas."[7] "Du trauerst" reads "Knabe, deine *Blicke* trauern!"[8] Wulfrin does not call Palma; "sein *Blick* rief Palma."[9]

It is not enough to single out the eye; Meyer is even more precise and focuses attention on the pupil of the eye — "Zur Erde starrt' sein *Augenstern*"[10] — or on the corner of the eye,[11] on the eyelash, on the eyelid, on the eyebrow. Pescara finds the stains of travel on Victoria: "Aber deine edeln *Lider* sind ja noch ganz bestaubt."[12] "Und er forschend zu dem Bild sich neigte"[13] reads in the final version, "Wie den Fund

man dem Gelehrten zeigte / Der die graue *Wimper*
forschend neigte."¹   Perseus views the sleeping
Medusa: "Wenn nur die blonde *Wimper* schlummern
bliebe."² Cäsar Borgia expresses disgust: "Dem Va-
lentino netzt die *Wimper* sich . . . / Pfui! Ist das eines
Weibes *Augenlid*?"³ Unlike the simple expression of
emotion in Heine's phrase, "Ich grolle nicht," Meyer
localizes the "Groll" in the *Brauen*, which are, in
turn, definitely fixed on the *Stirn*: "Der Manlier*stirn*
verzogne *Brauen* grollen."⁴ The chief obstacles in the
way of matrimony for Meyer's Diana are her "hohen
und oft finstern *Brauen*,"⁵ which can be both scornful
and forbidding. In fact, small and apparently insig-
nificant parts of the eye, like eyelashes, eyelids, eyebrows, play an important part in revealing emotion
in Meyer's characters, as can be readily discerned
from the frequent occurrence of the words *Wimper*,⁶
Lid,⁷ *Brauen*.⁸

In this manner Meyer's eye envisages concrete objects, selects parts of the body, singles out a certain
definite feature, focuses attention exactly on a precise
portion of that feature, the characteristic point, the
punctum saliens, which can stand for the whole as a
pars pro toto. One can, as a matter of fact, construct a
complete anatomical figure from this series of illustrations taken from his stories, beginning with
Schulter and *Brust* and continuing to the *Hand*, with
its *Faust, Finger, Fingerspitze, Fingerbeere*, to the
Fuss, with *Sohle, Ferse*, sometimes represented by

Sandale, to the *Kopf* with its *Gesicht, Antlitz, Miene, Züge*, which features are again separated into *Wange, Stirn, Nase, Nasenspitze.* Similarly the *Mund* has its *Lippe, Mundwinkel, Gaumen*; the *Kinn* its *Bart.* The *Ohr* is not so prominent as the *Auge* with *Augenwinkel, Augenstern, Blick, Lid, Wimper, Braue* frequently occurring.

Other writers of course try the same device, not always to the same degree nor always with the same effect. I think for example of George Meredith, even more mannered at times than Meyer, with his "Wilfrid lifted an *eyelid*,"[1] or "Mr. Adister peered into his *brows*,"[2] not to omit mention of the famous description in *The Egoist*: "And, says Mrs. Mountstuart, while grand phrases were mouthing round about him: 'You see he has a *leg*.' That you saw, of course. But after she had spoken you saw much more."[3] I think of a modern imagist, who describes a slim, girlish figure with the line, "Your girl's body had no *breasts*."[4] I think of Detlev von Liliencron, writing, "Und vorgebeugten Leibes rasen, / In einem Strich die Pferde*nasen*,"[5] or of Richard Dehmel in his poem *Entladung*, in which "vierzig Nonnen*waden* mit dem Wirbelwinde ringen," or of the artificial phrases of Ernst Hardt's prize play, *Tantris der Narr*: "die steilen *Falten* rechts / Und links von Eurem *Mund* sind mir zuwider."[6] Finally, I call attention to the common employment of this device in the graphic conversation of the plays of the Irish dramatist

J. M. Synge: "when your *legs* is limping and your *back* is blue";[1] "But who'll pity Deirdre has lost the lips of Naisi from her *neck* and from her *cheek* for ever."[2]

Meyer's characters resemble him in their gift of a vivid imagination, a highly developed visualizing power, and an accurate memory which flashes images upon the inward eye. "Dann öffnete sich langsam *sein inneres Auge*" is true of Don Giulio[3] as well as of Meyer.[4] Another character reads "weniger mit dem leiblichen als dem geistigen *Auge*";[5] still another asserts, "Ich lese es im Dunkel auf den kasteiten Mienen."[6] Pescara's imagination conjures up a profusion of mental images, concrete, graphic, and precise. "Ich sehe den Aretiner . . . und höre ihn lästern. . . . Und ein faunischer Jubel. Der Aretiner lacht, dass er fast mit dem Stuhl überschlägt, er schüttelt sich, er lacht aus vollem Halse."[7] Wulfrin, though not an eyewitness of his father's death, feels himself well informed: "Dennoch habe ich mir seine Todesgeberde vergegenwärtigt."[8] "Habt ihr das Bild jener Stunde?" is the question asked a group of characters in reference to the death of Wulfrin's father by the *Richterin*. Their answers are prompt in coming: "Als wäre es heute" — "Ich sehe den Comes vom Rosse springen" — "Wir alle" — "Dampfend und keuchend" — "Du kredenztest" — "Drei lange Züge" — "Mit einem leerte er den Becher" — "Er sank" — "Wortlos" — "Er lag."[9]

The accuracy and vividness of this visual memory

is not unusual in the characters of Meyer's stories, in all of whom there is a good deal of Meyer, "même dans ce vilain Morone," as he himself confessed.[1] The following characters have an acute power of visualization like him: Astorre, Don Giulio, Louis XIV, Madonna Olympia, Morone, Pescara, Poggio, Waser, Wulfrin; like him, they are ready to seize upon the salient feature which represents the person. "Lass ihn!" cries one, "Es ist Grumello! Ich kenn' das *Loch im Hut*!"[2] They believe with him that it is more convincing to show than to speak, that seeing is believing, and that actions speak louder than words. Gertrude's avowed intention of becoming a nun has not killed hope in the heart of her lover, but seeing her actually losing her hair as she takes the veil will bring the truth forcibly home to him, she feels: "Sieht er meine Flechten fallen, so hilft ihm das, mich vergessen."[3]

We believe what we see, especially what we see people do. The writer who wishes to stir the imagination should therefore not restrict himself to portraying people at rest, but should try to present them in action. Lessing, it will be remembered, believed that the remedy for lifeless description was the introduction of action. He cites Homer, who solved the problem of effective description by translating the coexistence of things into the consecutiveness of language[4] by giving description in terms of action, an artistic device in praise of which he does not tire.[5] The

action who shift their position. Meyer is thus able to present to the reader a whole series of pictures following one another in rapid succession.

The result is description in terms of action, a narrative of verbs. In treating the nobility, the compression, the precision of Meyer's style, we have already observed that his language was preëminently the language of verbs. Further illustrations can therefore be reduced without loss to one example from Meyer's prose: "Es *wohnte* in meinem Geiste. Es *begleitete* mich allgegenwärtig, *schwebte* in meinem Gebete, *strahlte* in meiner Zelle, *bettete* sich auf mein Kissen";[1] and one from his poems:

> . . . Eine *hebt* das Schwert und *zieht's*
> Und *lacht* und *haut* und *sticht* und *wundet*
> Licht und Luft.[2]

"Ich will die Exempel nicht häufen," as Lessing says; I merely select these two descriptions in terms of action, poetic pictures which would call forth Lessing's praise; these examples of verbs of motion or action which Scherer found "die poetischsten Redetheile,"[3] and which the modern experimental psychologist tells us tend to provoke an especially vigorous reaction, since they induce actual muscular movements of a more or less rudimentary form.[4]

Not content to make merely visual appeal, Meyer makes motor appeal in addition. Often he combines the two. When the ordinary person says, "Where

Gertrude is to become a nun," or perhaps employs a faded metaphor, "Where Gertrude is to take the veil," Meyer writes, "Wo morgen die Gertrude ihre *Hüften* mit dem *Strick umgürtet* und ihre *Blondhaare* unter der *Scheere fallen.*"[1] Becoming a nun does not remain a mere abstract concept; we are invited to observe the process, to watch the novice Gertrude, standing passively while her blond hair falls after the scissors' snip, and to follow her action as she takes the veil and encircles her waist with the cord which will bind her to the nunnery forever. Ezzelin, speaking normally, might well say, "If I had not done so and so, Diana would have been married and Astorre would be still a monk." Speaking in the language of Meyer's Dante, he says, however, "Hätte ich mein Ross nicht an einem gewissen Tage und zu einer gewissen Stunde längs der Brenta jagen lassen, Diana wäre standesgemäss vermählt und *Dieser hier murmelte sein Brevier.*"[2] "This one here, you see," he seems to say, pointing perhaps to the monk Astorre, and possibly placing his hand on his shoulder, "this one here would be standing not as he now stands before you but in a monk's cowl, with head shaved, and face bowed in devotion, his lips murmuring the breviary prayers." "When I first saw her" is an expression not suited even to the simple style of Meyer's Swabian *Armbruster*, Hans. Even he, whose speech is much less complex than that of Meyer's Dante,[3] becomes something of a stylist too, apparently preferring verbs of action to those of condition, combining visual with motor appeal when he says: "Zur Zeit, *da ich das Knie vor ihr bog*, hatte sie. . . ."[1] Speaking in person, Meyer himself writes, "Noch lag der hilflose Knabe in den Armen seines Kanzlers, als ein greiser Kämmerer *den Rücken vor ihm bog* und feierlich das Wort sprach";[2] similarly Wulfrin commends Arbogast's graphic account, not by saying, "Arbogast, der mir den *Tod* des Vaters," but "Arbogast, der mir das *Zusammensinken* des Vaters beschrieben hat."[3]

In discussing visual appeal in Meyer I have already had occasion to discuss at length Meyer's careful attention to concrete objects, in particular to definite parts of the body, especially the face and its features. I turn now to a discussion of these parts of the body in action, the play of features, the gestures of the characters, *Mienenspiel und Gebärdensprache in C. F. Meyers Novellen*.[4] Meyer feels that Romance influence encouraged him in his use of gestures. To Kögel he remarked, "Was ich nun vom Romanischen bekommen habe, ist, kurz gesagt, der Sinn für die Gebärde, die Geste." "Das ist nur Hang zur romanisch ausgebildeten Gebärde, und zur plastischen Darstellung," is his reply to the suggestion that his prose stories betray aptitude for the drama.[5] D'Harcourt, showing interesting examples of the "influence générale de Mérimée et de la littérature française sur Meyer,"[6] finds that "ici encore Mérimée a été le maître de Meyer."[7]

Of Ariosto,[1] who appears as a character in *Angela Borgia*, Meyer remarks, "Alles was er dachte und fühlte, was ihn erschreckte und ergriff, verwandelte sich durch das bildende Vermögen seines Geistes in Körper und Schauspiel";[2] and of Morone in *Die Versuchung des Pescara* he writes, "Er setzte diese Scene fort: jedes Wort des Zwiegespräches wiederholte sich in seinem Ohr und selbst jede Miene und Gebärde desselben bildete sich ab in seinen Zügen und schwang in seinen Muskeln fort."[3] "Ihr massloses *Geberdenspiel*"[4] is characteristic of all Meyer's figures, who are endowed with both "bewegtes *Geberdenspiel*"[5] and "bewegliches *Mienenspiel*,"[6] to use Meyer's own phrases.

"*Geberde*, Teufel, dich nicht allzu wild!"[7] is the warning in *Hutten*; "*Gebärde* dich nicht wie ein Rasender"[8] the warning given to Morone, who is cautioned "sein ausschweifendes *Gebärdenspiel* . . ."[9] zu mässigen,"[10] for as another character suggests, "Ich kann nicht sprechen, wenn eure *Gebärden* so heftig dareinreden."[11] Like the youth in *Plautus im Nonnenkloster* these characters possess "in *Geberde* und Rede . . . viel natürlichen Anstand";[12] like the Moorish story-teller in *Der Heilige* they know how "die *Geberde* beider Geschlechter und jeden Alters und Standes mit beweglichem Mienen- und Gliederspiele darzustellen."[13] Don Ferrante of *Angela Borgia* is apparently not the only one among them "[der] eine starke schauspielerische Ader hatte."[14]

It is instructive, as d'Harcourt suggests,[1] to keep
statistical count of the number of times Meyer uses
the word *Geberde*, and this labor of compilation has
more recently been done in part.[2] How impressive it
is to pass in review the imposing array of references to
Geberde which Meyer's poems[3] and prose[4] represent, may be observed from the selected lists here reprinted in the notes. "Dum tacent, clamant."

It is more interesting, however, to contemplate the
nature of the gestures employed and the use to which
they are put. It appears that Meyer's characters are
not restricted merely to the conventional gestures of
everyday life, such as nodding the head in assent[5] or
shaking it in refusal,[6] placing the finger on the lips to
signify silence,[7] pointing to the object discussed,[8]
lifting the hands in deprecation,[9] dismissing a servant
with a wave of the hand,[10] shaking the fist to show
anger,[11] though it is worthy of comment that even
gestures such as these find their way frequently into
Meyer's poetry and prose. It is a mistake to assume
that this is a method of sense appeal exclusively in the
possession of the dramatist, that it is only the actor
on the stage who has it in his power to convey very
vividly by his gestures the effect of a situation on him
and to evoke that effect in the audience.[12] To be sure,
a writer of prose stories or poems only rarely makes
the most of the method, as Meyer does when he
creates characters whose mobility of countenace, variety of facial expression, and facility of gesture re-

veal decided dramatic tendencies which better suit
actors on the stage than characters in prose narrative.
To show anger, in Meyer's stories just as on the stage,
a character clenches his fist, shakes it at his adver-
sary, seizes his sword, tears his books to tatters and
scatters the remnants to the winds, dashes down his
cup from the table and treads it under foot: "Erbost
stiess er den Becher von der Bank und setzte den
Fuss darauf."[1] To show contempt a man spits at the
cloister which he despises as he rides by.[2] When he
submits a petition he kneels; when he laughs he must
needs hold his sides: "Die Gräfin hielt sich den
wackelnden Bauch."[3]

Meyer's characters are not restricted, however, to
these traditional gestures. They are never at a loss
for the proper facial expression or appropriate gesture which befits the occasion and which is the correct accompaniment to their speech or emotion: "Mir
schaudert vor der Zelle! und sie machte eine *Geberde*,
als risse oder wickelte sie sich eine Schlange vom Leibe
los";[4] "Steht ab von Eurer Laune! und er machte die
Geberde, als griffe er einem Rosse in die Zügel, das mit
einem unvorsichtigen Knaben durchgegangen ist."[5]
The miser in *Die Hochzeit des Mönchs* "machte die
Geberde eines Krämers, der Gewichtstein um Gewichtstein in eine Wagschale legt."[6]

The dramatist Grillparzer under date of 1817 jots
down, "Als Cromwell das Parlament aufhob, zog er
seine Uhr aus der Tasche und warf sie auf den Boden,

dass sie in Stücke zersprang. 'Ich will euch zer-
schmettern wie diese Uhr!' rief er dabei aus. Wie mag
bei dem Zerschellen der Uhr am Steinpflaster den
Parlamentsherren das Herz gezittert haben! Etwas
Ähnliches müsste auf der Bühne von der herrlichsten
Wirkung sein. So Wort und Bild zu gleicher Zeit!"[1]
Similar effects Meyer attains in his stories. Franz
Sforza, pointing to Bourbon, whom he accuses of
coveting his beloved Mailand, is not made to wait for
his answer: "Da schmetterte Bourbon, als zerstöre er
sich selbst, mit einem zornigen Wurf sein krystallenes
Glas an den Marmorboden, dass es mit schrillem
Misston in Scherben zerfuhr. 'Hoheit,' rief er, 'da
liegt mein Fürstenthum Mailand!'"[2]
So the men of Meyer's stories, much like actors on
the stage, accompany their thoughts and emotions
with expressions of the face and movements of the
body which aid in revealing their state of mind. They
supplement their thought and their speech by action,
illustrating their statements with a gesture. With
them, words and action coalesce. They suit the action
to the word, giving, in Grillparzer's phrase, "So Wort
und Bild zu gleicher Zeit." Thus Poggio: "'Ich ent-
schuldigte mich mit der, Freunde, Euch bekannten
Kürze und Schwäche meiner Arme.' Der Erzähler
zeigte dieselbe mit einer schlenkernden Geberde."[3]
So Franz Sforza: "'Ihr Alle, selbst Dieser da' — er
blickte wehmüthig nach seinem Kanzler — 'habet
immer nur euer Italien im Sinne, und ich gelte euch'

— er blies über die flache Hand — 'soviel!'"[1] Similarly Jürg Jenatsch: "ohne mich um irgend einen
Einspruch so viel zu kümmern! Und er blies leicht
über die Fläche seiner Hand hin."[2] So Boccard:
"'Nichtig ist das, wie dies Gebilde meiner Finger!'
und er schnellte das Brotmännchen in die Höhe."[3] So
the fool in *Die Hochzeit des Mönchs*: "'Aber,' reizte
der böse Narr, 'das Kind ist gewachsen, so hoch!'
Er hob die Hand. Dann senkte er sie und hielt sie
über dem Boden. 'Und die Kutte Eurer Herrlich-
keit,' grinste er, 'liegt so tief!'"[4]

Actions speak louder than words. Before Angela
Borgia can give answer to the question put to her,
Cardinal Ippolito bends to pick up a chain loosely
woven of blades of grass that has just fallen from her
hands. "Wie diese Ringe verkettet sich Absicht mit
Absicht, um Euch zu kuppeln, Angela Borgia; aber
wie ich Euch kenne und liebe, werdet Ihr diese Kette
zerreissen, wie ich dieses nichtige Geflecht!"[5] Especially in moments of tense excitement the spoken
word is supplemented by gesture far more expressive. The Cardinal loses his self-control: "'Wer sagt
Dir, Bube,' wüthete er, 'dass ich sie tödten werde!
Was hindert mich, dies hier,' er packte mit beiden
Fäusten den Purpur über seiner Brust, 'in Fetzen zu
reissen und Angela als mein Weib an das Herz zu
drücken?'"[6] Pescara makes a sombre, symbolic, but
very graphic statement of his aim: "Da sprach es zu
ihm: 'Was ist dein Ziel, Avalos?' Er erblickte Mon-

cada. Der Feldherr griff mit der Hand in das erlo-
schene Kohlenbecken, schloss sie und streckte sie
gegen Moncada. 'Mein Ziel?' sagte er und öffnete die
Hand: 'Staub und Asche.'"[1]

Gestures thus supplement speech; sometimes they
even take the place of speech. In *Pescara* we read of
two characters: "Ihre dringende und flehende Gebärde wollte sich in Worte verwandeln,"[2] but they
did not get as far as words: "Da schloss ihnen
Pescara den Mund." This is typical, for on occasion
Meyer's men dispense with words altogether and per-
form a pantomime. Meyer does not let Ascanio say
outright that a man is addicted to drink. He writes
instead, "Er — Ascanio krümmte den Arm, als leere
er den Becher — und hernach wird er tiefsinnig oder
händelsüchtig."[3] Meyer's characters do not make a
mere verbal threat to kill a man, they prefer a more
direct indication of intention: "'Euer!' lockte er,
'wenn ihr Don Giulio' . . . Firlefanz machte die Gebärde des Erstechens: 'Abgemacht, Eminenz!'";[4]
"'Den Giorgio Jenatsch!' lachte der Italiener wild
und stiess sein Messer in einen neben ihm liegenden
kleinen Brotlaib, den er Herrn Pompejus vorhielt
wie einen gespiessten Kopf an einer Pike. Bei dieser
nicht zu missverstehenden symbolischen Antwort";[5]
"Da blies der Waffenmeister in die Luft und ich
verstand, Herrn Heinrichs Seele sei von hinnen ge-
fahren."[6]

These gestures must be understood, for often we

have only the gesture and nothing else. It is not uncommon to demand no word from a character of Meyer but only a silent reply, as in the poem:

> Sage Ja . . . mit einem Wink der Lider . . .
> Und vom Scheiterhaufen steigst du nieder![1]

For many of the characters on occasion depend entirely on what in Becket is termed "die edle Beredsamkeit seiner *Geberde*,"[2] which we must be able to grasp when words fail: "Ich stand zu ferne um ihre Worte zu verstehen, aber ihre *Geberden* sprachen deutlich genug."[3] Speech is not of so much consequence, but we must note gestures: "Seine *Geberde* aber war,"[4] and understand them: "Sie *verstand* die *Gebärde* und ging ihres Weges."[5]

So much depends on the proper interpretation of gestures that in two of Meyer's stories, *Die Hochzeit des Mönchs* and *Plautus im Nonnenkloster*, the whole action may be said to hinge on the interpretation of a pantomime, Astorre on the bridge in the one case, Poggio in the chapel in the other. In *Hutten*, in the section entitled "*Die Geberde*," Gemmingen conveys an important message to the hero by means of a gesture;[6] in *Die Hochzeit des Mönchs*, finally, the gesture of the tyrant Ezzelin, as he waves a greeting to a boat "mit einer weiten *Geberde*,"[7] not only causes the boat to capsize but starts the action toward the catastrophe with which the tragic story concludes.

"Und nicht genug an Geschrei und *Gebärde*,"[8] we

must have the more subtle play of features and all the
fine niceties of facial expression. The reply to the
question, "Was sagte er denn?" reads, "Zuerst zog er
die feinen Brauen zusammen."[1] That is almost as
important a part of the reply as the actual words
spoken to the delicately adjusted characters of
Meyer's creation, who so much resemble him. Meyer
confided to Kögel that he liked to dictate to a secre-
tary because "Sein verstehendes oder nicht verstehendes Auge macht mich aufmerksam wenn ich . . .
eine Gebärde ausgelassen, also einen Sprung in der
Reihe der bewegten Gestalten gemacht habe."[2] So
sensitive was Meyer to the effect of facial expression
in others, so careful are the characters created by him
to watch the facial expression of their fellow actors.

Meyer's characters, good actors all, possess grace of
gesture and mobility of countenance. The features, of
which he is so uncommonly fond, are represented in
play to express emotion. The corners of the mouth
twitch or turn up or down, the eyelids are lifted or
lowered, the eyebrows are raised or contracted,[3] the
eye itself reflects the soul. Like Pfannenstiel in *Der
Schuss von der Kanzel*, Meyer's men are all deeply
moved "von der Sprache dieser Augen,"[4] by the faces
and features of their fellow characters, and with good
reason, too. For with Meyer, as with Lavater,[5] face
and heart are identical. The features are the index
of character.[6] Thus the "vormalige Stallmeister, der
Sohn eines Schenkwirths und einer Dirne, den ein

knechtischer Ehrgeiz und ein eiserner Wille emporge-
bracht" must have "einen plumpen Körper und das
Gesicht eines Bullenbeissers, denn Stirn, Nase und
Lippe waren ihm von demselben Schwerthiebe ge-
spaltet."[1] A change in character is reflected in a
change of countenance: in the case of Del Guasto,
"Mit der Weichheit seiner Züge aber verlor er auch
die Liebenswürdigkeit seiner Seele. Das schöne Profil
bekam einen Geierblick und den immer schärfer sich
biegenden Umriss eines Raubvogels";[2] in the case
of the King of England, "Statt des freudigen Leuch-
tens von ehemals gab es [sein Angesicht] nur noch
einen matten weissen Schein von sich, wie faules Holz
in der Nacht."[3] We must see, indeed, how even the
passing emotion of the moment is immediately reflected in the face: "Das feingeformte Haupt mit
seinen wenigen schneeweissen Locken lag auf dem
roten Kissen mit geschlossenen Augen, aber dem
wachen Ausdruck des Triumphes über seinen ge-
lungenen Anschlag";[4] "Das gestorbene Antlitz trug
den deutlichen Ausdruck triumphirender List."[5]

Little wonder that Meyer's characters are all
adept at reading faces, for the features speak.[6] Thus
"[Moncada] suchte in der Miene des Feldherrn zu
lesen."[7] Schadau of *Das Amulett* has no need to hear
the words of the fanatic denouncing the Hugenots, for
by searching the faces of the auditors, which is synon-
ymous with searching their souls, he realizes the
dangerous ground on which he stands.[8] Morone ap-

proaches the sleeping Pescara "um das schlafende
Antlitz zu belauschen, ob nicht die jetzt willenlose
Miene die verschwiegenen Gedanken abbilde und
ausdrücke."[1] "Der verlorene Mönch, Serapion, lau-
erte auf den Heimkehrenden, um die Mienen desselben zu erforschen und darin zu lesen, was Astorre
über sich beschlossen hätte."[2] Poggio says of himself,
"Ich schickte einen schrägen Blick auf die im Halbdunkel sitzende Novize, die Wirkung der drei Orakels-
spiele aus den Mienen der Barbarin zu lesen."[3]
Meyer remarks, "Die Marquise las in den veränder-
ten Zügen des Arztes, dass sein Zorn vorüber und
nach einem solchen Ausbruche an diesem Abend
kein Rückfall mehr zu fürchten sei."[4] Only of "le bel
idiot" in *Das Leiden eines Knaben* do we find "Der
Knabe deutete meine erstaunte Miene falsch."[5] He,
like the lunatic Olympia of *Die Hochzeit des Mönchs*,
who interprets a gesture falsely, deserves pity for his
lack of acute perception and, like her, meets misfortune. Only the stupid and crazed characters in
Meyer's stories appear incapable of comprehending
correctly the speech of facial expression.

This sensitiveness of the characters in Meyer's
stories to the features of their fellows is but another
means which Meyer employs in the presentation of
his persons. The actors are portrayed through the
medium of their fellow players, quite in the manner
advocated by Lessing, who commends Homer's device in giving an idea of the beauty of Helen by show-

ing the effect of her appearance on the Trojan elders:
"Was Homer nicht nach seinen Bestandtheilen be-
schreiben konnte, lässt er uns in seiner Wirkung erkennen,"[1] a procedure heartily approved by more
modern aestheticians, who note that the poet gives
effective descriptions "[dadurch] dass er den Ein-
druck, den der Gegenstand auf einen Betrachter
macht, uns mitfühlen lässt."[2] This is the method of
Meyer, who said, "Personen schildere ich möglichst
nur so, wie sie den Mithandelnden erscheinen."[3]

Employing such a method, Meyer can very well
dispense with long descriptions of characters and
avoid detailed enumerations which were once the
prevalent method of portraying places and persons in
poetry.[4] Boileau scoffs at the poets who interrupt the
course of a narrative to indulge in a lengthy description of a palace and its grounds; "I skip twenty pages
to get to the end of it all," he says, "and then escape
with difficulty through the garden."[5] Lessing, direct-
ing his *Laokoon* at this school of descriptive poetry,
unequivocally condemns the long descriptive poems
in imitation of Thomson's *Seasons*, "die frostigen
Ausmalungen körperlicher Gegenstände,"[6] for which
his contemporaries showed such inordinate fondness:
"Was das Auge mit einmal übersieht, zählt er uns
merklich langsam nach und nach zu, und oft geschieht
es, dass wir bei dem letzten Zug den ersten schon
wiederum vergessen haben."[7] His sentiments are
echoed by Herder — "Auch ich hasse nichts so sehr,

als tote stillstehende Schilderungssucht, insonderheit,
wenn sie Seiten, Blätter, Gedichte einnimmt"[1] —
and by all modern aestheticians who demonstrate by
psychological experiments the futility of the inventory method of description of persons or places.
Meyer introduces his characters quite regularly
with a very brief descriptive notice, quite in accordance with Lessing's "Regel . . . von der Sparsamkeit
in den Schilderungen körperlicher Gegenstände."[2] We
find, for example, "ein Kriegsmann von treuherzigem
Aussehen, Germano mit Namen, der einen Ringelpanzer und einen lang herabhangenden Schnurrbart trug";[3] "mein neuer Beichtiger hat keine
Schönheit und Gestalt: eine Art Wolfsgesicht und
dann schielt er";[4] "voran auf einem schwarzen
Hengst ein Reiter in Scharlach, von dessen Stülphute
blaue Federn wehten, der jedem Kinde bekannte Jürg
Jenatsch."[5] Meyer is accustomed to give just a few
traits which the reader can readily assimilate "ohne
sich anzustrengen," as Lessing would say. Like a
painter he sketches in an outline, blocks the figure
out, and later lets the character fill in the frame himself, the method with which we are already familiar:
"plastisch greifbare Gestalten hervorzuzaubern und
sie handelnd auftreten zu lassen."

In these brief descriptions of character he is careful
to make the most of little, in accordance with the
principle of the modern aesthetician. Jonas Cohn, for
example, writing on *Die Anschaulichkeit der dichter-*

ischen Sprache and commenting on proper methods
of describing characters, says, "Der erste Satz dient
dazu, die Richtung des Verständnisses vorzuschrei-
ben. Sie gibt die determinierende Tendenz für die
anschauliche Erfassung der eigentlichen Schilder-
ung."[1] He would have found apt illustrations of this
procedure in Meyer's stories. Thus Hans, the *raconteur* in *Der Heilige*, is very fond of stating his own personal reaction to the characters for the benefit of his
auditor and his readers: "Als ich auf Schloss Wind-
sor zum ersten Male vor den König von Engelland
trat, zitterte mir das Herz im Leibe, denn er war von
gewaltigem Wuchs und herrischer Geberde und seine
blauen unbeschatteten Augen brannten wie zwei
Flammen."[2] "Zitterte mir das Herz im Leibe" is a
subjective touch which serves an artistic purpose. So
of another character: "Drinnen verkehrte mit dem
ihn *misstrauisch betrachtenden* Meier ein hagerer ge-
harnischter Gesell, der mir erst den Rücken zuwandte, dann aber mitten im Gespräche rasch den
Kopf drehend, gerade in der Richtung des Schlöss-
chens, den scharfen Haken seines Raubvogelge-
sichtes zeigte. *Ich erkannte den Geier. . . .*"[3] Thus
Meyer himself describes Cardinal Ippolito: "Verzehrt bis zur Entkörperung, leichtgebückt, mit
durchdringenden Augen unter der kahl und hoch ge-
wordenen Stirn, *schien er lauter Geist zu sein*, grausam
und allwissend,"[4] and so encourages in the reader the
desired reaction toward the character.[5]

Descriptions of places, like those of people, are brief, reduced to a minimum, and always made to serve a definite purpose. The descriptions of setting and background, fairly frequent in *Jürg Jenatsch* or *Die Richterin*, disappear almost entirely in *Die Hochzeit des Mönchs*. In *Pescara* and *Angela Borgia* descriptions of nature are done in a few strokes. In *Pescara* "Das offene Fenster füllte ein glühender Abendhimmel";[1] "Es war nach einem leuchtenden ein trüber Tag. Kein Windhauch und nicht der leiseste Versuch einer Wolkenbildung. Keine Lerche stieg, kein Vogel sang, es dämmerte ein stilles Zwielicht wie über den Wiesen der Unterwelt."[2] In *Angela Borgia*, "April kam und überschüttete Ferrara mit Blüten";[3] "Die Lenznacht war schwül und mit dem Dufte unzähliger Blüthen beladen."[4]

Nature is, however, always completely in accord with the action. In *Der Heilige* the stage is carefully set for the unfortunate meeting of the main characters. "Es war an einem grauen Tage und auf einer trübseligen Heide, dass die Herren zusammentrafen."[5] After the failure of the meeting the weather becomes even more depressing, "Als wir die graue Heide, den Ort des verweigerten Kusses, verlassen hatten und schweigsam in uns gekehrt nach der festen normännischen Stadt Rouen trabten, trieb uns nach einem warmen, verlängerten Spätherbst eine rauhe Winterluft die ersten Flocken entgegen. Mich drückte der Kummer wie ein zu enger Brustpanzer, denn ich gab die Sache meines Königs verloren. . . ."[1]

The background of nature, the *milieu*, the setting
with its statuary and paintings, to all of these Meyer
attaches symbolic significance. In this fastidiousness
in arrangement of detail we may discover one of the
reasons why he never wrote the dramas which he so
ardently desired to compose. He was not content
merely to remain the dramatist who writes the play.
He wished also to usurp the place of stage manager
who sets the stage, arranges scenes, costumes, colors,
and groups his people. He wished to regulate the
scenery and the lighting, to direct the music, so that
soft music might sound out when occasion demands.
So the choir of nuns chants an appropriate requiem in
Pescara; the "dies irae, dies illa," is conveniently
wafted to the ears of the characters at an opportune
moment in *Die Richterin*. He could not very well en-
trust this careful arrangement of the scene to an ordinary *régisseur*, any more than he could expect the
average actor to reproduce all the subtle changes in
gesture and facial expression by which he himself
could reveal a thousand different moods.[2]

With fastidious care Meyer selects furniture, dec-
orations, works of art, plastic and pictorial, for the
background and setting of his stories, and at times
attaches almost too much symbolical significance to
them.[3] In *Der Heilige* Hans sees Richard, the king's
son, trying to effect a reconciliation between his father
and the chancellor: "Herr Richard neigte sich über

die blasse Hand des Kanzlers und benetzte sie mit Thränen kindlichen Dankes. Wahrlich, auch mein Herz jubelte, dass die erbarmungswürdigen Leiden meines Königs zu Ende gingen. Da musste ich, wehe, über den Häuptern der Zweie ein steinernes kleines Scheusal erblicken, das, auf dem Gurt eines Pfeilers hockend, mit seinem Krötenbeinchen höhnisch nach ihnen stiess und dazu die Zunge reckte. Dieses missfiel mir, obschon es ein Zufall war, and ich hätte die beiden Herren lieber erst am nächsten Pfeiler sich scheiden sehen, wo ein harfenirender Engel seine Schwanenfittige ausbreitete."[1]

The rupture between king and chancellor in the same story has a similarly symbolic repercussion in art. When the chancellor announces his intention of deserting the king, "erstaunte mein Herr und König und erschrak in den Tiefen seiner Seele. Das Staatssiegel entglitt seiner Hand und fiel klirrend auf den Marmorboden. Ich trat hinzu und bückte mich nach dem kostbaren Geräthe, dessen Griff von purem Golde war. Als ich es prüfend besichtigte, siehe, war es zersprungen und eine feine Spalte lief mitten durch den edeln Stein und das Wappen von Engelland!"[2]

When we find Meyer representing the militaristic instincts of a character earlier described as "ein leidenschaftlicher Liebhaber von Geschütz — Ganz Kanone"[3] by having him fashion soft bread at table into the form of a small cannon: "Der Herzog, der eben aus weichem Brot ein kleines Geschütz knetete,"[1] we may perhaps be impressed by the exploitation of this possibility for characterization. When symbolical significance attaches to the dessert at the dinner table as well, as in *Pescara*, "so merkt man Absicht und man wird verstimmt." ... "Zwischen Eis, Früchten und Naschwerk erblickte er eine von seinem Zuckerbäcker kunstvoll geformte Mandelkrone. 'Siehe da,' scherzte er, 'etwas für meine ehrgeizige Victoria!' Er bot sie ihr, deren Herz zu pochen begann."[2] In his zeal "plastisch greifbare Gestalten hervorzuzaubern," Meyer here conjures forth a cannon of soft bread, a crown of almond paste, whose precise forms shall serve as concrete symbols of abstract ideas. In so doing he becomes, here and elsewhere, the victim of his own exacting principle, "Genug ist nicht genug!"

Just as the profusion of pictorial detail in a work of art results very often from inability to create plastic forms, so the exaggerated external decoration of Meyer's stories seems to have its source in his congenital inability to visualize objects in contours and colors. "Er bekannte die Fähigkeit des Plastisch- und Farbigsehens von Hause aus gar nicht oder nur im geringem Grade besessen, vielmehr dieselbe sich allmählich erworben zu haben," his friend Frey relates, pointing out how Meyer endeavored by conscious and repeated efforts to envisage scenes in the colors of pictures and with the contours of plastic art.[3] Baumgarten feels that this effort was due to an instinctive and unconscious striving for compensation: "Meyers Streben nach sinnlicher Plastik ist ein instinktiver Versuch, den Mangel an innerer Plastik zu ersetzen."[1] It seems, therefore, that Meyer's effort to create "Concrete Forms and Moving Figures" may have resulted from the same powerful urge for compensation which the next chapter discusses in detail under the title "The Principle of Polarity."

IV

CONCLUSION

1. THE PRINCIPLE OF POLARITY

Vollkommnes will auch ich erstreben —
Ich selbst kann nicht vollkommen heissen,
Drum will ich's keck dem Stein entreissen.

OF the problems presented by the complex personality of Conrad Ferdinand Meyer none
seems more puzzling than the tremendous contrast
between the passionate, forceful world of the Renaissance created by his imagination and represented in
his stories and the picture of timidity and impotence
produced by his own image, as reflected in his letters
or contained in contemporary accounts of his life and
character. To the humdrum daily round of the
middle of the nineteenth century in which he and his
contemporaries moved his creative imagination preferred the more glorious and colorful era of the Renaissance with its emphasis on will and action and its
possibilities for free expression and full development
of personality. His artistic fancy peopled his stories
of this great period with strong and stalwart men of
action, magnificent personalities, exalted martyrs or
individualistic, self-willed, scheming, and unscrupulous criminals. Many if not all of these characters

form a rather startling contrast to their self-effacing, pious creator with his mild, gentlemanly manner and his shrinking, modest reserve, a man of whom conscience had made, if not a coward, at least a person of moral scruples who lacked the daring enterprise, the purposeful energy, and the brutal courage of those colossal criminals who cause the conflict and catastrophe of his predominantly tragic stories.

This contrast between Meyer's own nature and that of most of the characters he created has been frequently observed. Some of the more recent critics have attempted to explain this pronounced and apparently irreconcilable polarity in his production. Among them Linden, correctly distinguishing between opposite types of characters in Meyer's stories, calls the one type, best represented by Jürg Jenatsch, "aesthetisch-konkret," and the other, best represented by Thomas Becket, "ethisch-abstrakt,"[1] terminology which recalls Meyer's own description of his uncompleted *Komtur*: "Kampf und Gegensatz des humanistisch-aesthetischen und des reformatorisch-ethischen Princips."[2] Correct as he is in fixing this important contrast not only in certain characters[3] but also throughout Meyer's life and work,[4] Linden makes a mistake, it seems to me, in assuming that Meyer, reserved, timid, and unemotional, had a heart aglow with the same fire which animates his heroes of the Renaissance, and that he wears a mask merely to conceal the passionate emotion surging within.[5] Nor

does Meyer in my opinion resolve these opposing conflicts in himself or in his work and achieve the synthesis which Linden would call the compelling law of his
life.¹ Meyer did not, even in the secure days of his
comparatively successful maturity, display the domi-
nant personality of his more enterprising and energetic characters as Linden would have us believe:
"Auch in Meyer selber lebt von nun an die sin-
nenstarke Weltfreude, der Persönlichkeitswille, die
Energie seiner Jenatsch und Astorre, seiner Stemma
und Vittoria Colonna: denn welcher Dichter hätte je
eine vollkräftige, von blühendem Leben erfüllte Gestalt in seinen Werken hingestellt, die nicht seiner
eigenen Natur entsprang und tiefstes Fühlen seiner
Seele wiedergab?"²

The very question shows Linden's lack of understanding of a principle which the earliest German
philosopher termed "coincidentia oppositorum" and
more recent German psychologists call ambivalence
and which, if properly applied, may yield a solution
of the problem of Meyer's polarity. For I prefer to
agree with the remark of Erich Everth, "Diese coincidentia oppositorum, mit Nicolaus von Kues, dem
ersten deutschen Philosophen, zu sprechen, ist eines
der Geheimnisse des Künstlers C. F. Meyer."³
Robert Faesi phrases the whole matter more simply
still by saying that works of the creative imagination may be either "das Abbild oder das Ge-
genbild ihres Schöpfers."⁴ It seems clear that in his

writings Meyer portrayed both himself and his opposite, both the reality of his own life and the realm of
his desires and dreams, both the world in which he be-
longed and the world for which he longed. If he appears to depict by preference and more prominently
the lands and times of his longing rather than his own
age and actual place of residence and to present characters who are his opposites rather than those created
in his own image, he does so perhaps because during
a large part of his secluded and inactive early life
dreams had played a more important rôle than cruel
reality, and art had become a substitute for life. For
poetry is not merely, as Linden seems to feel, the
mirror of a poet's experience; it can also become life's
complement, supplying what reality refuses to yield.[1]

Where life failed him Meyer fled to art; when the
present disappointed he sought refuge in the past;
from the smallness of his own time and country he
turned to the spacious epoch of the Italian Renaissance where he found the fulfillment of his longing for
color, variety, and grandeur: "Auch tentiren mich
jetzt — trotz meines sehr reellen Schweizer Patriotis-
mus — die grösseren ausländischen Stoffe weit mehr
— es ist eine Art Reiselust."[2] As we travel to find
more congenial and pleasant surroundings, hoping for
a change for the better, so Meyer leaves behind him
the small times and stodgy atmosphere of mediocrity
"mit der grossen Historie zu fahren," as he remarked
to Keller.[3] His confession to Rodenberg is even more

revealing: "Das Mittelmässige macht mich deshalb so traurig, weil es in mir selbst einen verwandten Stoff findet — darum suche ich so sehnsüchtig das Grosse."[1] He felt he could realize this longing better outside of his time and outside of himself, illustrating Thomas Mann's definition of longing: "Wohin die Sehnsucht drängt, nicht wahr? Dort ist man nicht, — das ist man nicht,"[2] and Jakob Burckhardt's summary of greatness: "Grösse ist, was wir nicht sind."[3] This historical past gives him "ein eigen beruhigendes und grossartiges Gefühl";[4] the characters of the Renaissance are for him "an sich schon Poesie."[5] In portraying historical characters of distant times in his prose he accomplishes the same purpose as in the selection of statues as subjects for his poems; both become symbols of something which he longs for but cannot realize, and from which he may derive a feeling of greatness, repose and perfection:

> Vollkommnes will auch ich erstreben —
> Ich selbst kann nicht vollkommen heissen,
> Drum will ich's keck dem Stein entreissen.[6]

The world of longing which his imagination created to supply the lack in his own life is peopled with strong and heroic characters who possess qualities complementing rather than resembling his own. In a letter to Meyer, Louise von François, contrasting these heroes to the "marklosen Gesellen neuerer Novellisten," remarks, "Ihre Helden können was sie

wollen. Ihr Problem ist nicht die halbe Kraft, sondern eine doppelte."[1]   R. M. Meyer also observes,
"Starke Naturen sind alle seine Helden, allen ist die
Seele übervoll von aufgehäuften Kräften, Begierden,
Regungen."[2]   It remained, however, for d'Harcourt,
whose primary interest in Meyer as he once assured
me was predominantly a psychological one, to discover the reason for Meyer's preference for these
strong men of action: "Meyer a cherché dans son
œuvre un complément de lui-même: faible, il nous
a donné des caractères de force, contemplatif, des
êtres d'action."[3]   Meyer himself confesses his love of
contrast to his own character, his attraction to resolute personalities stronger than his own. Speaking of
Laube, he writes to Louise von François, "Mir, der
ich meine Gegensätze liebe, war sein Realismus und
sein resolutes Wesen stets höchst angenehm."[4]   In
life Meyer leaned on resolute people, like Wille and
Ricasoli, and felt himself attracted by the manly,
soldierly bearing of his father-in-law Colonel Ziegler,
and of his dearest boyhood friend Conrad Nüscheler,[5]
who became an officer in the Austrian army. In
women also it was the virile, masculine element that
most appealed to him, whether in his sister Betsy or
in his friends Mathilde Escher and Louise von François.[6]   It is not surprising therefore that in his works
he portrayed forceful characters; enterprising women, — Gasparde, Gustel, Lucrezia Borgia, Rahel,
Stemma,[7] — and energetic, ruthless, almost violent

men, — Astorre, Jenatsch, Henry II, Frederick II,[1]
— all *Ausnahmemenschen, Kraftmenschen, Ueber-
menschen*, in whom he admired the energy and force
of character which he did not possess. He seems to
have spoken from his heart when he incorporated in
Die Hochzeit des Mönchs the reflection, "Denn das
Höchste und Tiefste der Empfindung erreicht seinen
Ausdruck nur in einem starken Körper und in einer
starken Seele."[2] So he became "un rêveur de na-
tionalités; ce débile avait besoin d'appuyer sa fai-
blesse à de grands événements et à de grands pays."[3]
In politics he approved Bismarck: "Ich gehe mit ihm
durch dick und dünne";[4] in the drama, Shakspere,
writing of his own stories, "Ich schakespearisiere darin
ein bisschen, nach Kräften, versteht sich."[5] In keeping with these enthusiasms he created heroes of large
stature like Jenatsch, of whom he boasted, "J'ai la
certitude que ce n'était qu'un coquin et j'en ai fait un
personnage."[6] In similar manner and for the same
reason the poets of the Munich school contemporary
with him composed their tragedies about great
heroes and heroines of legend and history. Geibel
wrote his *Brunhild*; earlier, Hölderlin had admired
Napoleon; and later, Nietzsche, neurasthenic and
neurotic, invented the superman and the blond
beast.[7]

Everything great and heroic, whether offered by
the colorful personalities of the Renaissance as portrayed by Burckhardt, or as typified by Bismarck in

the contemporary diplomacy of his own day, was
welcome to Meyer as a release from the commonplace
atmosphere of his own democratic country and a refuge from the memory of his pitiful youth, the experiences of which apparently never ceased to trouble
him. It becomes more and more apparent that it is
impossible to comprehend Meyer without careful consideration of the two serious crises coming over him
at the ages of twenty-seven and sixty-seven which
virtually enclose in a frame the productive years of
Meyer's life.[1] The first of these, La Crise de 1852–
1856,[2] which without d'Harcourt's volume of letters
with that title might have remained "la période la
plus mal connue de l'existence de C. F. Meyer,"[3]
helps materially to explain the later polarity in
Meyer's personality and literary production. Born
into a family of cultivated tradition and of neurasthenic parents,[4] Meyer suffered from an unfortunate
heredity that produced nervous crises, from the first
of which he recovered only after a seven months'
sojourn in the sanatorium of Préfargier.[5] It was un-
pleasant that he should have heard his mother com-
plain of him, as Betsy reports, mentioning him as no
longer among the living;[6] it was a still greater shock
to his sensitive nature to hear himself constantly referred to as "der arme Conrad,"[7] sometimes even as
"das verruckte Conrädli."[8] The contempt of his
former comrades already established in professions
while he himself was not only unsuccessful but sick as

well[1] and the tactless remarks of his troublesome
mother[2] made him completely miserable.[3] This
misery of his lost youth remained for long as a sort of
psychic trauma so that he never liked to mention in
conversation the time of which his verses tell:

> Ich war von einem schweren Bann gebunden.
> Ich lebte nicht.   Ich lag im Traum erstarrt.[4]

His feeling of inferiority was prolonged because he attained only late in life those outward signs of success
in sex, profession, and society which the symbols of
his troubled dream of earlier days clearly reveal him
as desiring.   "Denke dir," he told his sister one morning, "mir träumte, ich sass in einer Kutsche, hatte
eine Frau und einen Schnurrbart."[5]   His moustache
did not flourish until he was forty, he found a feminine
consort to share his carriage and company only at
fifty.

For these reasons he preferred to conceal from himself and others the portion of his early life which was
so unfortunate.[6]   When he began to compose he
selected the form of the historical *Novelle*, as we remember, "parce qu'elle me *masque* mieux."[7]   To another friend he makes further explanation: "Wahr
kann man (oder wenigstens ich) nur unter der dramatischen *Maske* al fresco sein."[8]   The occurrence of the
word *Maske* here and frequently elsewhere[9] is in itself indicative of his love of mummery and masquer-
ade.   He accordingly conceals rather than reveals

himself in the large majority of his characters, in whom it is difficult to discover direct traces of his personality. In an early work like *Das Amulett* it is comparatively simple, nevertheless, to detach certain autobiographical traits from the character of the hero. Like Meyer, for example, his hero Hans lived for long as a recluse, suffering depression because of his inactivity and because he was regarded as "ein junger Mensch ohne Verdienst." Aside from his lessons in fencing, in which he, like Meyer in his youth, indulged, he had few contacts with society in his small town, the provincialism of which appalled him. When he arrived in Paris as a provincial he resembled Meyer again in his timidity in the presence of women, his moral revulsion at certain indecencies in French works of art, and more important still, in his finally awakening on French soil to life, which is not unlike Meyer's own experience.[1] In a later story, *Das Leiden eines Knaben*, Meyer confessed that he had treated situations and sentiments of his own unhappy and unfortunate youth;[2] in regard to *Pescara*, as we have heard, he writes, "Dans tous les personnages du Pescara, même dans ce vilain Morone, il y a du C. F. M."[3] In this story, however, as in general elsewhere, it is almost less difficult to find portrayal of his opposite than direct revelation of his own character.

Beside the characters like Jenatsch, Henry II, Morone, Lucrezia Borgia, who may be said to repre-

sent antipodes to Meyer's personality developed from
his desire, stand their opposites, who more closely resemble their creator, Herzog Rohan, Thomas Becket,
Pescara, and Angela Borgia. Together with the more
active masculine women typified by the "Wild-
fang"[1] Gust Leubelfing, who masquerades as a man
to act as *Gustav Adolfs Page*, there are also more passive feminine types like Lucia in *Jenatsch*, Grace in
Der Heilige, Antiope beside Diana in *Die Hochzeit*,
Julia Dati beside Vittoria Colonna in *Pescara*. Their
outlines are extremely delicate, however; their forms
remain shadowy and indistinct; they play comparatively minor parts in the action, scarcely opening
their lips in speech.[2]

To all critics this contrast of characters in Meyer's
stories and the resulting conflict of motives has been
clear. Long before Linden had developed the contrasting terms "aesthetisch-konkret and ethisch-abstrakt" to apply to Meyer's heroes, d'Harcourt had
called to mind the characteristic dualism between
affirmation of life and renouncement of life incorporate in the title to a section of the collected poems,
Frech und Fromm, which, according to him, dominates Meyer's life and work.[3] This contrast and conflict of opposites is sometimes fairly concrete and
specific: between historical movements, Renaissance
and Reformation; between representative cultures,
Southern-Romance and Northern-Germanic; between religious worlds, ancient-pagan and modern-

Christian; between religious beliefs, Catholic and Huguenot. These conflicts are indications of a more general struggle between freedom and determinism, individuality and fate, life and death, the finite and the infinite; between concern with the world of the noisy present with its willful passions, dramatic excitements, disturbed movement, and absorption in the realm of the quiet past in devout contemplation, resigned reminiscence, and unperturbed rest, as symbolically represented in *Pescara* by the statues of Presenza and Assenza.[1]

What has not been so clearly realized by critics, however, is that in this general polarity between sensual indulgence and austere denial, sensuous aestheticism and moral asceticism, unscrupulous cruelty and inhibitions imposed by conscience, between assertion and resignation, Meyer was portraying his opposite and himself, the conflict in his own breast. In contrast to his own passive morality, his impotence and weakness, his delicate refinement, he created many active and some very immoral characters who display vigor and vitality, strength which approaches brutality and does not shrink from crime, people who have all the qualities which he does not possess. This portrayal of himself and his opposite, this tension between the poles of his own world and the world of his longing, becomes the one great theme of his prose narratives, of which the individual stories are merely variations.[2] There is, therefore, more expression of personality in his works than at first appears if we appraise the frank, elemental, wilful people who freely indulge their full-blooded impulses as characters created by his longing and desire, who form a fairly satisfying surrogate for what life had in reality refused to offer him.

One of Meyer's favorite books, his sister records,[1] was the autobiography of Benvenuto Cellini, which he read more than fifty times, apparently intoxicated by the account of the tremendously powerful and pragmatic personality who dared to act and who realized concrete results. Not even the cruelty of this gay, naïve, and energetic nature displeased him. He was carried away by the action of the narrative, by the mere movement in the life of this man, so little introspective as to be interested only in facts. The same unwillingness to concern himself with the formless figments of introspective imagination which so much troubled Meyer himself he attributes to his Ariosto: "Ihm aber schauderte vor dem Verharren in solcher gestaltlosen Tiefe. Alles was er dachte und fühlte, was ihn erschreckte und ergriff, verwandelte sich durch das bildende Vermögen seines Geistes in Körper und Schauspiel und verlor dadurch die Härte und Kraft der Wirkung auf seine Seele."[2] It seems to me inappropriate to generalize on the basis of this remark, as Linden does, to the effect that this is a fundamentally unromantic characteristic of Meyer's classic nature.[3] It is far better to interpret Meyer's preference for external objects as a protection against the chaos of his inner life, as a refuge from himself.[1] He apparently envies this ability to work off inner troubles by interest in externals. Cellini and Ariosto most probably attracted Meyer because of their power to convert ideas into facts, thoughts into action, desires into result.

Any art which owes its origin to a desire to escape life, to forget reality, naturally tends to concern itself with the opposite of actual experience. In order to get rid of the feeling of shortcoming and inferiority, one dreams of persons and circumstances that one resembles only in imagination. These imagined people very often represent in extreme degree the qualities lacking in one's own personality. Some of Meyer's heroes, for example, like Jenatsch, Henry II, and Astorre, pursue their one-sided policy to such extremes that they resort to force and crime only to meet misfortune and invite destruction for themselves and others. Wulfrin even imagines there are no limits to his transgressions: "Ich bin der Schrankenlose."[2] It may be, too, that some of the unwarranted outbursts of brutal emotion which occur from time to time in Meyer's stories are a similar release for his pent-up, primitive impulses. Everth, after recording several of these violent *Ausbrüche*, appears unable to make a satisfactory explanation except the one implied in his question, "Brauchte er solche Stellen als Ventile, um sich dann wieder desto sicherer zu fassen?"; that is, a tendency for which he elsewhere employs the term *Abreaktion*.[1] After considering the contribution which Meyer's inventive imagination made to the motives of his historical narratives, which include seduction of a minor daughter by her father's friend (*Heilige*), breaking of a monk's vow (*Hochzeit*), violent murder of husband and lover (*Jenatsch, Richterin*), adulterous love of a judge for a criminal (*Angela Borgia*), incestuous desire of a brother for his sister (*Richterin*), one is tempted to agree that "der in strengster Zucht lebende Meyer hat die unzüchtigste Phantasie." Meyer's pronounced preference for brutality in the themes of his stories may result from "Verdrängung" which encourages this "Bewunderung des Schwachen für das Brutale."[2]

Tender-hearted like Schiller's brigand Karl Moor of whom Amalia could maintain, "Nicht eine Fliege konnt' er leiden sehn,"[3] the same Meyer who revels in brutal outbursts of passion, violent lust, and cruel and bloodthirsty crime is extraordinarily tender to cats, dogs, and pigeons, which he keeps as pets,[4] and also to beetles and butterflies that he encounters in the outdoor world. To his sister he confides, "Ich stehe mit der kleinen Tierwelt auf dem besten Fusse. Käfer, Eidechsen, Schmetterlinge wissen es wohl, sie haben mir vieles zu danken. Ich habe ihrer manchem das Leben gerettet."[5] Among them he can afford to be altruistic and merciful.

His sister is unable to comprehend why her brother, whose fancy flooded his stories with full-blooded people, is repelled by temperamental personalities in real life. "Wie kam es nur," she inquires in discussing two such characters, "dass die . . . Dichterseele meines Bruders gerade bei der Berührung mit diesen beiden Poetennaturen sich in den hintersten Winkel seiner inneren Abgeschlossenheit flüchtete und verbarg? Er, der sonst den lebendigen Blutstrom des Temperaments an andern hoch wertete und seine eigenen Gebilde damit zu durchfluten und zu erwärmen bestrebt war?"[1] In general Betsy Meyer confesses that in reality her brother was uncomfortable in the presence of stormy personalities and careful to avoid violent conflicts and emotional shocks: "Mit überfeinen, reizbaren Gefühlsorganen ausgestattet, wehrte er heftige Eindrücke und stürmische Persönlichkeiten, so gut er konnte, von sich ab. Er schätzte und bewunderte bewusst leidenschaftliches Auftreten nur, solange er es studieren konnte. Ihm persönlich mangelte jede Fähigkeit dazu. . . . Starken Konflikten — 'Szenen,' wie er das nannte — waren seine Nerven nicht gewachsen. Heftige Auftritte, schmerzliche Erschütterungen verletzten ihn tief."[2] It appears, therefore, that Meyer's preference for his opposite in his stories can be best explained by the law of ambivalence, by his longing for what he himself did not possess in life. Perhaps he is speaking of his own desire for compensation and the polar attraction characteristic of him when he allows Angela Borgia to confess to Giulio, "Gerade deine viele Sünde, die ich strafen muss, ist es, die mich an dich kettet."[1]

Not even when he attempts to portray his opposite in art, however, does Meyer produce splendid pictures of triumph. More and more the characters become afflicted with his own faults. They are grand, to be sure, as he would have them, grand in their dreams and desires, but more superb in succumbing than in triumphing, marked for defeat rather than victory, overcome not by *hybris* but by their own shortcomings. Not radiant and unafraid like the German hero Siegfried, they resemble him, however, in their one vulnerable spot. Like Pescara, they have within themselves their secret mortal wound which renders them beyond temptation, which keeps them from acting in confident defiance and from achieving final victory. Not unlike Grillparzer, therefore, Meyer portrays characters who act in life only to learn that action also leads but to the grave.[2] The contradiction in Meyer's own nature, torn as it was between concrete assertion and abstract resignation, between sensuous desire and austere conscience, becomes characteristic of his heroes. He reveals himself and them when he admonishes Hercules Strozzi, "Dein strenger Rechtssinn verdammt das, was Dein Auge beglückt und das Feuer deines Herzens entzündet. Das ist Dein Widerspruch und Dein Irrsal."[3] In his youth a thin, scrawny neurotic, who impressed persons variously as an actor, a Catholic priest, or a Prussian officer,[1] Meyer became a corpulent family man with the appearance of self-assurance and prosperity as if he were in reality as decided and aggressive as the heroes of his stories.[2] Behind this portly exterior he remained, however, uncertain and undecided, not unlike the *Amtsbürgermeister* Meyer of Chur, whom he describes in *Jürg Jenatsch* as of imposing appearance: "Bei näherer Betrachtung jedoch verrieth die Befangenheit des gewöhnlich gesunden und ruhigen Gesichts und der bängliche Ausdruck der irrenden Augensterne einen geheimen Widerspruch seines Innern mit der magistralen Sicherheit seiner vollkommenen Haltung."[3]

This secret contradiction remains in Meyer's soul even though in art he found an outlet for his longing and as an artist found the happiness he had not experienced as a man, rejoicing like his Fingerhütchen, who through invention of a rhyming line is relieved of his ugly hunchback.[4] Just as he was able to live only through his polarity, so his characters also like him are torn, undecided, and dualistic, reflecting "seinen eigenen Lebensprocess."[5] For Meyer did not succeed in resolving this antithesis; he never achieved complete harmony and synthesis,[6] nor did he ever create an harmonious character in whom this fundamental conflict was resolved. In fact his desire for the great, the heroic, the well-rounded, the unified, the harmonious and complete is merely the longing for compensation that would complement his character and supply the qualities he lacked; in a word, his works appear to be the very symbol of the principle of polarity which dominates his life and dictates the form and content of his production.

2. THE ATTAINMENT OF FORM

Ich will nicht in Manier verfallen,
sondern in der Natur bleiben.

It is not surprising that a form of art resulting from "The Principle of Polarity" and produced by "The Struggle for Expression," deliberately intent on attaining "The Grand Style and Manner," and obviously, almost obtrusively, striving to conjure forth "Concrete Forms and Moving Figures," should betray the labor which brought it forth and bear traces of artistic artificiality in its composition. Nor is it remarkable that Conrad Ferdinand Meyer himself as a self-conscious and reflective artist with an introspective temperament and sensitive nature should have been among the first to find defects and detect flaws in his own productions. When he depicts in his verses the temptation of luxuriant decoration besetting the architect of a cathedral,

> Wollt' ich in schwelgendes Verzieren,
> In üppig Blattwerk mich verlieren,
> Und opfert's nicht mit keuschem Sinn
> Dem Ganzen streng ich zu Gewinn,[1]

he is merely describing dangers which he endeavored to avoid, but to which he too sometimes succumbed. Impressed with the solemn seriousness of his charge, he tries his best not to toy or trifle with his art. He sets out with the idea of letting the whole dominate the parts, ready to sacrifice sternly and in chastity individual elements of decoration and display. Nevertheless he frequently loses himself, as we have seen, "in schwelgendes Verzieren, in üppig Blattwerk," with which he adorns his highly ornate Renaissance façades. Realization of this shortcoming is apparent when he informs Rodenberg of his resolve to write *Die Richterin* "ohne Adjektive und ursprünglicher als den überladenen Renaissance Mönch."[1] In this same letter he seems not only to have realized with Voltaire that "l'adjectif est l'ennemi du substantif,"[2] but also that his earlier Renaissance story, *Die Hochzeit des Mönchs*, lacks spontaneity and appears overornate and studied. For this reason he will make an effort to become more elemental and primitive, "ursprünglicher." Even earlier he had felt a lack of naturalness and the presence of mannerism in his production. During work on *Pescara* he writes, "Ich will nicht in Manier verfallen, sondern in der Natur bleiben."[3] Despite the fact that he abhors "die Breite, die sogenannte Fülle"[4] he tries to combat his tendency to brevity and epigrammatic compactness: "Ich möchte meiner Kürze entgegen arbeiten, welche sonst leicht mit den Jahren überhand nehmen könnte."[5]

Perhaps he is portraying certain tendencies toward
artificial over-refinement of manner in his own character and art when he says of Papst Clemens in his
Pescara: "Er schärfte . . . den Stift so lange, bis zu
seinem Aerger die allzufeine Spitze abbrach."[1] As a
matter of fact Meyer often sharpens down a point so
fine that it finally breaks off, forgetting that he can ill
afford to let fastidiousness degenerate into a fault
without forfeiting at the same time spontaneity and
natural vigor. He attains perhaps by his stylistic
devices "the highest degree of elegant and pregnant
implication," but it is the most serious defect of his
style that he has been unable to accomplish this result "unobtrusively." In this important respect he
does not approach the perfection of style of which
Stevenson speaks: "That style therefore is the most
perfect which attains the highest degree of elegant
and pregnant implication unobtrusively."[2]

These general criticisms of Meyer's manner, many
of which he himself anticipated, may be summed up
by saying that in his love of decoration and ornament
he becomes at times the victim of the motto of his
poem, "Genug ist nicht genug . . . Genug kann nie
und nimmermehr genügen."[3] To censure him for certain mannerisms in such gentle terms seems a form of
criticism all too mild to many of the most bitter
enemies of his art. To one among them Meyer seems
"der Mann der Maske," "der brokatne Zürcher,"

"ein Lebensscheuer und Lebensschwächlicher," "der in gipserner Monumentalität schwelgt."[1] Another condemns his works as being "nicht aus Marmor, sondern aus Marmorersatz"[2] and calls attention to the man "der Meyers einstürzende Gipsfiguren ganz in den Sand streckte," Franz Ferdinand Baumgarten.[3] In crisp and facile epigrams Baumgarten himself rapidly disposes of Meyer's heroes: "Meyers Helden stehen etwas traurig wie Zuschauer beiseite. . . . Sie spielen mit dem Leben, weil sie nicht mehr mitspielen im Leben. . . . Meyers Menschen sind gebrochene Naturen. . . . An die gebrochenen Naturen schliessen sich an die schwachen und fast pathologischen Menschen. . . . Meyers Menschen sind Einsame, Fremde und Kranke. . . . Sie sind späte Enkel. Sie sind ein Ende. Meyers Helden haben keine Söhne."[4]

In no less summary fashion does Baumgarten dispatch Meyer's stories: "Das Merkmal der Meyerschen Novellen [ist] eine fast schmerzende Plastik der Teile und eine mehr dekorative als organische Einheit des Ganzen. . . . Die Novelle *Die* [*sic*] *Leiden eines Knaben* ist die Tragödie der Schwäche, *Die Hochzeit des Mönchs* ist die Tragödie der Haltlosigkeit. . . . Meyers Novellen haben keine organische Gestalt, nur eine dekorative Form. . . . Sie sind gebaut, nicht gewachsen. . . . Meyers Novellen . . . sind dekorative Kunstwerke."[5] Meyer's poems Baumgarten pronounces "Erfahrungen und nicht Gefühl.

... Er dichtete seine Erinnerungen, nicht seine Erlebnisse. ... Die Gedichtsammlung ist ein Buch der Bilder und kein Liederbuch."[1]

Meyer himself Baumgarten ruthlessly exposes to view as an unemotional, nervously timid man, unheroically hiding behind an artist's mask, posing in empty, aesthetic impotence as the monumental poet of the Renaissance: "Conrad Ferdinand hat nie einen Freund und nie eine Geliebte gehabt. ... Er verkehrte viel mit Kunstwerken und wenig mit Menschen. ... Leidenschaft hat Meyer nie erlebt und im Leben nie gesehen. Nur in Museen hatte er Helden im Bilde geschaut. ... Und dieser lebensfremde, leidenschaftslose und furchtsame Neurastheniker wollte gerade das leidenschaftlichste Leben, das Leben der historischen Helden schildern! ... Meyer intellektualisiert die Renaissance. ... Meyer stilisiert den Renaissancestil. ... Meyer ist der Dichter des Renaissancismus."[2]

The storm of protest and discussion "über und um Conrad Ferdinand Meyer"[3] which this most drastic and destructive of attacks on Meyer's style and personality has stirred up has resulted in a wholesome clarification of critical opinion. Although the startling aphoristic formulation of his findings may have made Baumgarten seem to some a second Nietzsche crying for "eine Umwertung aller Conrad Ferdinand Meyer-Werte," most recent criticism has remained more or less unmoved by the sound and fury

of his bitter indictments.¹ If one discounts the brutality of his broadsides one finds that the more construc-
tive of his critical remarks result in an appraisal of
Meyer not far removed from that sponsored by Meyer
himself and represented in the preceding pages of our
portrayal of the style and the man.² This is particularly true of Meyer's poetry, on which Baumgarten
had earlier produced an article from which his book
was later developed,³ as we may observe if we now
attempt a final appraisal of Meyer's accomplishment
in poetry and prose.

Gottfried Keller, esteeming Meyer most highly as a
poet, admired especially the form of his verses. Toward the end of the year 1881 he wrote to Theodor
Storm, "Meyers Bedeutung liegt in seinen lyrischen
und halb epischen Gedichten. Wenn er sie einmal
sammelt, so wird es wahrscheinlich das formal
schönste Gedichtbuch sein, das seit Dezennien erschienen ist."⁴ Storm's reply after the volume of
Meyer's poems had appeared denies Meyer's claim to
be considered a lyric poet: "Wenn Sie aber früher
meinten, der Band werde eins der formell schönsten
*Lieder*bücher werden, so werden Sie jetzt, wo es vor-
liegt, wohl anders denken: Ein Lyriker ist er nicht;
dazu fehlt ihm der unmittelbare, mit sich fortreis-
sende Ausdruck der Empfindung, oder auch wohl die
unmittelbare Empfindung selbst."⁵ Storm had included no poems of Meyer in his anthology,⁶ probably because he failed to find in them those qualities

of emotional immediacy which in the famous *Vorwort* to the volume he made the test of lyric excellence. "Richtig ist, dass man in vielen, vielleicht der Mehrzahl, noch die Arbeit fühlt" is his later comment on the volume.[1]

Among the moderns even so friendly a critic as Adolf Frey finds Meyer's poetry, like his prose, possessed of "wenig Gegenwart, sondern wesentlich nur verklärende Rückblicke. Es fehlt ihr die Jugend. . . . Zwar fehlt ihr fühlbar Jugend, Leidenschaft und das Liedermässige."[2]   Robert Faesi notes, "Nicht den Augenblick, den Rückblick dichtet C. F. Meyer, nicht die Gegenwart, sondern die Vergangenheit — die eigene wie die der Völker."[3] Both of these conservative and rather more conventional Swiss critics are therefore in substantial agreement with the judgment that Meyer's poems are *Bilder* and not *Lieder*, which Baumgarten formulated in such an epigrammatic, paradoxical, and extreme manner.[4] Meyer himself, finally, gives a similar clue to the proper approach to his poetry. As an announcement to accompany the volume of *Romanzen und Bilder* he suggests to his publisher the following: "Tiefe der Empfindung, künstlerische Gestaltungsgabe, Reinheit der Form sichern diesem kleinen Band gewählter Gedichte einen sympathischen Leserkreis."[5] Of the earlier volume, *Zwanzig Balladen*, Betsy Meyer reports to her brother the judgment of a friend, Frau Pfizer: "Im ganzen findet sie bei Dir ein bedeutendes Talent

zweiten Ranges. . . . Ein begabter Mensch ist Conrad sicherlich . . . aber es fehlt ihm doch der 'Hauch,'
an dem man den geborenen Dichter erkennt."[1]

If his poems lack immediacy of emotional appeal,
being based on reminiscences rather than on actual
sensuous experiences recollected in tranquillity, if
many of the verses betray the labor spent on them,
they offer as compensation the merits of compact
form and powerful concentration of expression, main-
taining such uniformity of excellence that the entire
volume contains scarcely one poem inferior in form.[2]
Among the poems many readers find the ballads best,
all of which are elevated in language, compressed in
form, tense in situation, dramatic in treatment. Over
all the verses hovers a fine autumnal fragrance rather
than the natural freshness of spring. They hold out
not so much attractive hope to youth as mild comfort to maturity. First collected and published in one
volume in 1882 when Meyer was already fifty-seven
years old, his verses are not the spontaneous and in-
spired outpouring of youthful ardor. They do not resemble fresh flowers, fragrant with the air of spring,
which have burst from the bud into bloom, but in
their rich, autumnal flavor are rather to be compared to slowly ripened fruit, maturing and mellow-
ing in the autumn of life, falling like a ripe apple
with muffled sound to the ground. The first poem in
the volume, called *Fülle*, furnishes confirmation of
this metaphor:

Genug ist nicht genug! Gepriesen werde
Der Herbst! Kein Ast, der seiner Frucht entbehrte! —
Tief beugt sich mancher allzureich beschwerte,
Der Apfel fällt mit dumpfem Laut zur Erde.[1]

Always troubled with the feeling that his lyrics
lacked red blood and vital reality, Meyer represents
himself in the characteristic verses of the poem *Mö-
wenflug*. Watching gulls in flight and observing their
reflection mirrored in the water under them, he is
struck by the similarity and relationship between
"Trug und Wahrheit," "Schein und Wesen," and
searches his own soul:

Und du selber? Bist du echt beflügelt?
Oder nur gemalt und abgespiegelt?
Gaukelst du im Kreis mit Fabeldingen?
Oder hast du Blut in deinen Schwingen?[2]

Despite resemblances which Maync mentions between individual poems of Meyer and similar poems
of Uhland and Mörike,[3] it seems clear that Meyer's
poetry is little related to that of Uhland, Mörike,
Eichendorff, Lenau, or Heine, written in the tradition
of the German *Volkslied*, but belongs rather in the line
of formally correct verse under foreign standards
which runs in the development of German poetry
from Hölderlin through Platen to the modern symbolic poems of Stefan George. Here Baumgarten's
judgments seem most discriminating: "Meyers Weg
führt von der volksliedartigen Erlebnislyrik zur sym-

bolischen Lyrik. ... Meyers Lyrik steht am Aus-
gang der musikalischen Erlebnislyrik und am Ein-
gang der plastischen und der symbolischen Lyrik
von heute. ... Conrad Ferdinand Meyers plastische
und pathetische Stimmungslyrik der Verschwie-
genheit ist die Lyrik des intellektuellen, einsamen
Kulturmenschen: des repräsentativen Menschen im
ausgehenden 19. Jahrhundert."[1] As a "Kultur- und
Bildungsdichter" Meyer is a forerunner of the
moderns, Hofmannsthal and Rilke; as a symbolic
poet and master of rhetorical language, a predecessor
of Stefan George.[2]

In his prose as well as in his poetry it is the choice
and precious bouquet that attracts the connoisseur.
Rodenberg could write to him without too much
flattery, "Sie sind ein Kabinettswein, den man in
kurzen, vorsichtigen Zügen schlürft, damit nichts von
dem Aroma verloren gehe."[3] His historical *Novellen*
do not belong with the psychologically analytical
masterpieces of Gottfried Keller, nor with the charm-
ing lyrical *Stimmungsbilder* of Theodor Storm, his two
famous contemporaries in the field of the short story.
With more formal talent than inventive genius, more
artistic craftsmanship than naïve inspiration, Meyer
produced stories which stand as excellent examples of
polished prose such as Paul Heyse and his contemporaries of the Munich School tried but failed to
achieve, and which have remained to serve as models
in our day for such distinguished stylists in contem-

porary German literature as Wilhelm Schäfer, Ricarda Huch, and Thomas Mann.[1]

For the material of his historical *Novellen* Meyer did not engage first-hand in a study of the sources but remained content with secondary and usually very subjective accounts.[2] First in importance among such historians to whom he had recourse was Jakob Burckhardt, through whose eyes Meyer saw the Italian Renaissance.[3] In general Meyer regarded history, not objectively, but subjectively; his interest was not in the facts but in the forces underlying them, which seemed to him to be the same forces which were in contradiction in his own character and which form the eternal conflict of all historical development.[4] Between his reading of historical treatments and his poetical composition of the same material he commonly allowed five to ten years to elapse, during which period "meine bildende Kraft sich mit denselben beschäftigt."[5] This formative force of his own creative imagination is more important than pedantic accuracy in antiquarian detail. Never learned or slavish in following historical facts, he is guilty of historical inaccuracies and mistakes, which did not seem to trouble him. He felt, as he confessed to Kögel, that there were occasions, "wo der Dichter ergänzen darf."[6] He tells Georg von Wysz of the intentions of an historical character in a contemplated novel *Der Dynast*, which are "natürlich nicht geschichtlich, aber psychologisch und poetisch wahr."[7] To Louise von François he writes, "Ich behandle die Geschichte souverän, aber nicht ungetreu."[1] He confesses, finally, of the historical facts for his novel *Jenatsch*: "Après avoir lu à peu près tout ce qui a été écrit sur ce sujet-là, j'ai mis tout cela de côté et j'ai donné le champ libre, très libre à mon imagination. . . . Quant aux traits historiques — j'en ai disposé plus que cavalièrement."[2]

His historical narratives traverse almost a thousand years of European history, from the time of Charlemagne and the Carolingian Renaissance in *Die Richterin*, through the darkest days of the Middle Ages in England under Thomas Becket and Henry II of *Der Heilige*, down to the sunny seventeenth century of *le Roi Soleil*, Louis XIV, in *Das Leiden eines Knaben*. Meyer's main interests were centred, however, in the Reformation and its results in Germany, France, and Switzerland and even more in the Renaissance in Italy. *Die Hochzeit des Mönchs* plays on the threshold of the Italian Renaissance; *Plautus im Nonnenkloster* in the early fifteenth century; *Die Versuchung des Pescara*, finally, portrays the fine flower of the *Cinquecento* just before it begins to wither and fade. Although in the grand style, Meyer's pictures of this period portrayed in the German manner appear to cultivated French eyes not without traces of "Behaglichkeit zurichoise" and "Gemütlichkeit germanique."[3] More interested in his own ideas than in historical facts, Meyer was careful, moreover, never to represent as main characters the most distinguished personages of the different historical periods. When they appear they stand in the middle distance or keep in the background: Luther in *Hutten*, Gustav Adolf in the *Page*, Louis XIV in the *Leiden*, Frederick II in the *Hochzeit*, Charles the Great in the *Richterin*, and Charles V in *Pescara*.[1]

These grand heroes are very different in station and manner from the simple, unassuming Swiss burghers of middle-class life whom Meyer's more distinguished contemporary and fellow countryman Gottfried Keller was content to portray in his *Leute von Seldwyla*. The historical background of Meyer's stories extends only to the beginnings of the baroque, the very period in which Keller's historical treatments begin, to continue from there down to his own day. In fact we may term Keller's imagination and language, the form and content of his stories, characteristically baroque, because of their unwillingness to be bound within fixed confines, and thereby establish the essential difference between him and Meyer, whose aristocratic works, confined always within self-imposed limits, with their preference for large lines and comparatively undisturbed surfaces, in imitation of the calm harmony of ancient art, remain Renaissance in spirit.[2] This same difference between the detailed and the monumental, the naturalistic and the idealistic, the romantic and the classic seems to have motivated the general comparison of the "miscroscopic" Keller with the "telescopic" Meyer, originally made by Louise von François,[1] and the more specific statement of the modern critic, "Wenn Keller zuweilen an den Dürer des Rasenstücks und des Hasen erinnern kann, so Meyer an den Dürer der Apostel."[2] For where Keller wishes to bring objects close up to the eye so he can examine them as if with a microscope and portray them with the same realistic detail with which Dürer painted his patch of grass, Meyer removes the object to get the proper perspective and to show the large lines and majestic forms that resemble Dürer's monumental Apostles.

This is one important aspect of the customary comparison between Keller and Meyer which can produce more interesting results than the conventional eulogy of these everlasting Siamese twins of Switzerland and partners in the Swiss firm of "Keller und Meyer," as Keller once contemptuously remarked,[3] or the commonplace appraisal of Meyer as Switzerland's second-best poet, placed with, if somewhat after, her favorite and more favored son, Keller: "Gottfried Keller und — *longo sed proximus intervallo* — Conrad Ferdinand Meyer," in Erich Schmidt's rather superior phrase.[4] These two Swiss writers of the second half of the nineteenth century, contemporaries and compatriots, both born and resident in Zürich, both publishing poems but more important as writers of prose, both masters of the *Novelle* but failures in the field of the drama, which tempted them, form a contrast not unusual in the history of German culture,[1] whose dualism often produces contrasting contemporaries in different fields like Wolfram von Eschenbach and Gottfried von Strassburg, Dürer and Grünewald, Klopstock and Wieland, Goethe and Schiller, Beethoven and Mozart.

Alike in racial, these two Swiss poets are different in social origins: Keller is plebeian, democratic, content to remain provincial; Meyer, patrician, aristocratic, striving to appear cosmopolitan. The difference in taste resulting from their origins is reinforced by a difference in temperament: Keller is open, impulsive, tactless and uncouth; Meyer, reserved, cold, discreet and urbane. Taste and temperament dictate a point of view and attitude toward society: Keller remains republican and bourgeois, manifesting interest in the common weal and in the fate of his fellow man; Meyer, exclusive and reserved, isolates himself from society and keeps aloof from the men and problems of his time.[2] To adapt an idea from Keller's *Der grüne Heinrich*, we may say that whereas Keller himself took part in the march of events with an identification which we may designate as social, Meyer was content to watch the parade of men and time pass by, holding himself aloof as an individual.

The difference between this social and individual outlook on life reflects itself in their selection of subject matter and in the style of its treatment. Keller, playing a part in local politics, identifying himself with contemporary causes, selects subjects from middle-class Swiss society, which he treats in a human manner and humorous vein, producing a series of stories of which only one is tragic in outcome. Meyer, passing over middle-class subjects taken from contemporary Switzerland, from which he holds himself aloof in literature as well as in life, portrays events of the historical past of general European significance, treating persons of heroic stature and tragic destinies in stories of which only one fails to end in tragedy. For the atmosphere of idyllic simplicity that pervades Keller's tales of Swiss provincials and peasants Meyer substitutes an elevated solemnity in keeping with his historical heroes and sublime criminals. To the leisurely manner of epic discursiveness and careless completeness with which Keller recounts his narratives Meyer prefers compact, dramatic compression. With objective detachment he calmly calculates the artistic effect, coldly rejecting everything unimportant for his purpose, which is the moulding of his matter into final perfect form. So he avoids local words as well as provincial subjects in an elevated, polished style, which Keller felt resembled brocade; whereas Keller, on the other hand, exploited the possibilities of dialect flavor in his homely language and gnarled style, less like smooth, fine-grained, decorated Italian brocade than like ordinary, coarse, loose-woven Swiss homespun. Meyer feels that Keller's

discursiveness and didacticism, his tendency to teach
and preach, are characteristically Swiss, while he
himself spurns these republican preferences of his
compatriot, as a recorded conversation notes: "Keller
ist, was die Schweizer verlangen, lehrhaft, weit-
schweifig, er predigt. Das ist nötig, um den Schweizern
zu gefallen, es ist republikanisch. Meine grösste
Emancipation vom Schweizertum ist, dass ich das
nicht tue, dass ich es grundsätzlich vermeide."[1]

Never content to remain like Keller part and parcel
of German Switzerland, Meyer manifests a tendency
to emancipate himself from his own native background. This preference for foreign virtues, originally
an outgrowth of Meyer's inheritance and subsequent
training, was destined to cause one of the great conflicts in his life, never in my opinion altogether satisfactorily resolved. Inheriting French Swiss blood
from his mother, Meyer spent the formative years of
his life in the French part of Switzerland and in
France. In his brief and not very communicative
autobiographical sketch he points out: "So war mir
die französische Schweiz von jeher eine zweite Hei-
mat, wohin ich mich mehr als einmal geflüchtet habe,
wenn es mir zu Hause nicht nach Wunsch ging, und
immer mit gutem Erfolge. . . . So wurde mir von
jung auf die französische Sprache vertraut und ich
schreibe sie leidlich."[2] In a later letter to Haessel he
even feels that it is possible "dass mein Ohr feiner ist
für das Französische als das Deutsche, *geschulter* je-

denfalls."[1] Certainly there are more Gallicisms in his
German style than Swiss dialectic provincialisms.[2]
The emphasis which some nationalistic German literary historians place on the fact that Meyer was won
away from France for Germany by the war of 1870
and the formation of the empire in 1871 is misplaced
if it fails to mention Meyer's own version of the reasons for his choice. In a letter of January 16, 1871 he
writes to Georg von Wysz: "Auch ich habe meine
französischen Sympathien schwer überwunden; aber
es musste in Gottes Namen ein Entschluss gefasst
sein, da voraussichtlich der deutsch-französische Gegensatz Jahrzehnde beherrschen und literarisch jede
Mittelstellung völlig unhaltbar machen wird."[3] Describing himself ten years later in a letter to Keller as
"ein Gibelline . . . von jung an und . . . mehr als je,"[4]
he becomes enthusiastic about the German Empire,
its emperor, and its chancellor: "Als das deutsche
Reich wieder erstand, da erstand in C. F. M. der
Ghibelline."[5] But as late as 1890 he speaks of himself
as torn between two affiliations: "Et vaut mieux que
moi chassant de race. . . . Sachez que tout en étant
un semblant d'auteur allemand, j'ai conservé tout
mon goût pour la littérature française."[6]

As early as 1864 when Meyer's first poems appeared as *Zwanzig Balladen von einem Schweizer,* his
fatherly friend and French mentor Louis Vulliemin,
in a long review, declared that "une rare appro-
priation de la littérature française a communiqué à son

langage, comme à sa pensée, une netteté et une pré-
cision que l'on ne trouve pas souvent à ce degré dans
la poésie allemande."[1] Later Carl Spitteler, trying to
define *Die Eigenart C. F. Meyers*, remarks, "Je öfter
ich seine Novellen lese, desto unbedenklicher urteile
ich: das ist französisch, nicht deutsch, französisch bis
in den Bau des Satzes; wohlverstanden, nicht modern-
französisch, sondern französisch aus der klassischen
und vorklassischen Zeit. . . . Überhaupt möchte ich
die gesamte Kunstweisheit unseres Dichters, vor
allem sein eminentes Formgefühl auf französische Ur-
sprünge zurückführen."[2] Betsy Meyer loses patience
with such attempts to prove specifically French influence, which she calls "ein Missverständnis sehr ober-
flächlicher Art," and declares, "Die Franzosen haben
nie etwas anderes als eine urdeutsche Natur in meinem
Bruder erkennen wollen." She quotes her brother as
asserting, "Weniger französische als überhaupt ro-
manische Strömungen waren es, die mich beeinfluss-
ten."[3]

Louise von François applies to Meyer as also
to Gregorovius the play on words of her formula,
"Der nordische Sinn, gepaart mit südlichen Sinnen."[4]
D'Harcourt finds a real conflict in Meyer's attitude to the Latin world: "Mélange d'attraction esthétique et de répugnance morale: ce sera bien long-
temps l'attitude de Meyer devant le Latin, jusqu'à ce
que le domaine esthétique ait décidément, chez lui,
pris le pas sur le domaine moral."[5] Linden recognizes

the conflict between "Germanisch-romantisch-nord-
isch: das heisst Disharmonie, klassisch-romanisch-
südlich: das ist Harmonie," finding that "Meyers
Kunst ist zugleich südlich und nördlich, indem sie die
Disharmonien zur Harmonie zusammenzwingt. Sie
ist die Synthese einer Antithese";[1] but he is misled,
it seems to me, by his fundamental misconception of
Meyer's personality, which is not, as he appraises it,
strong, warm, and vital under a cold, lifeless mask, but
too weak and wavering to effect a synthesis of such
powerful opposing elements. Lusser[2] feels, as I do,
that Meyer is torn between two cultures, between
two opposite poles, Northern and Southern, Germanic
and Romance, Romantic and Classic, Baroque and
Renaissance.[3] Less sturdy Germans, to be sure, break
under the strain of this dualistic endeavor to unite
North and South: Hölderlin, standing between
Greece and Germany; Kleist, trying to unite the
drama of Sophocles and Shakspere; Nietzsche, at-
tempting to prove a connection between Aeschylus
and Richard Wagner, and to explain "the birth of
tragedy out of the spirit of music." Others end not
quite so tragically but still with synthesis unaccom-
plished and mastery incomplete: Grillparzer, Mörike,
Conrad Ferdinand Meyer.[4] The same problem con-
fronts us in the life of the most distinguished living
writer of German prose, Thomas Mann, rages in the
breast of his heroes and is even debated in his works,
which he is always ready to assert are characteristi-

cally German, perhaps on this very account. In this contrast and conflict Conrad Ferdinand Meyer resembles Thomas Mann and Thomas Mann's most characteristic hero, Tonio Kröger.[1] Like Tonio Kröger and his creator Meyer is "ein verirrter Bürger und ein Künstler mit schlechtem Gewissen," a dualistic nature, divided between two cultural ideals continually in conflict, which can be resolved in temporary and not completely harmonious compromise only after struggle. As the tired heir of an old family and an old culture Meyer, like Mann's heroes, is forced to contend with the congenital handicaps of physical and mental frailty. During thirty years of unremitting effort which testify to a resolute moral will and a surprising tenacity of purpose he overcomes most of these obstacles and wrests his artistic masterpieces from the muse despite the discouraging difficulty of the task. As an artist and as a man Conrad Ferdinand Meyer seems to me, therefore, eminently human, as if he exemplified the two lines which he prefaced to his *Hutten*:

"... ich bin kein ausgeklügelt Buch,
Ich bin ein Mensch mit seinem Widerspruch. . . ."

NOTES

NOTES

Note: Abbreviations referring to works by or about Meyer are explained in the bibliography. Other abbreviations occurring will be found self-explanatory.

3   1. *Vulgate*, John iii, 8; Baumgarten, 233.
    2. Goethe, *Sämtliche Werke*, Jubiläumsausgabe 38, 268.
4   1. Schopenhauer, *Sämtliche Werke*, ed. Grisebach, Reclam VI, 218, letter of September 3, 1815; Goethe-Jahrbuch, 9, 51.
    2. Meyer's most recent biographer, Maync, begins his chapter "Erlebnis und Dichtung," as Faesi before him had begun his book, with this statement of Meyer to his sister. Cf. Betsy Meyer, 139.
    3. Betsy Meyer, 45. Inaccurately cited by Everth, 9. Cf. Maync, 70.
5   1. Br., I, 138–139.
    2. Br., I, 411.
6   1. Cf. Bibliography, "Editions of Meyer's Works and Letters."
7   1. I have not neglected to familiarize myself with such general books on *Stilistik* as those of Ernst Elster, R. M. Meyer, R. Müller-Freienfels, *et al.*, to which my indebtedness in method is everywhere apparent; and with such specialized stylistic investigations of other authors like Grillparzer and Kleist, by A. Fries, G. Minde-Pouet, H. H. Stevens, *et al.*, to which references are given in the appropriate places; and finally, of course, with the work of former students of Meyer's style, one of whom, at least, seems to have employed at times a method similar to mine. Cf. Korrodi, 69, "Erst die Rückübersetzung in die konventionelle Prosa lehrt uns solche Zartheiten sprachlicher Kultur schätzen."

    After work on this investigation was already well under way, I was much encouraged to find that E. P. Morris, delivering the presidential address before the American Philological Association on "A Science of Style" (*Trans-*

actions, XLVI [1915], 103 ff.), advocated methods of stylistic analysis so closely resembling the method I have employed that I have allowed his general remarks to stand in my text.

8 1. The Swiss journalist Eduard Korrodi, in his *C. F. Meyer Studien* (Leipzig, 1912), loudly proclaimed Meyer some years ago as "einen Verächter der Dekoration," enthusiastically praising as excellent and effective the stylistic devices which later critics deride as faults. Where he finds exemplified in Meyer "Stileinheit," the sharper eyes of the German critic Franz Ferdinand Baumgarten detect "Stilverwirrung." In an annoyingly provocative and much-discussed book on *Das Werk Conrad Ferdinand Meyers, Renaissance-Empfinden und Stilkunst* (München, 1920²), Baumgarten, in contrast to Korrodi, is sure that "Meyers Novellen haben keine organische Gestalt, nur eine dekorative Form . . . eine mehr dekorative als organische Einheit des Ganzen." Among the numerous reviews of Baumgarten's book, which range from enthusiastic acclaim to drastic rejection, are:

E. Ermatinger, *Das Literarische Echo*, Jg. 19, pp. 847–851 (1917).

F. Ernst, *Deutsche Literaturzeitung*, Jg. 39, Nr. 33, pp. 715–717 (1918).

E. Everth, *Ztft. f. Aesthetik*, Bd. 13, pp. 77–97 (1918).

M. Hartenstein, *Preussische Jahrbücher*, Bd. 168, p. 304; Bd. 169, pp. 121–124 (1917).

A. Hauschner, *Börsen Courier*, Berlin, Nr. 333 (1920).

A. Heine, *Berliner Tageblatt*, 19, III, 1917.

Th. Heuss, *Neue Zürcher Zeitung*, 8, IV, 1917.

W. Heynen, *Deutsche Rundschau* (July, 1917), p. 135.

H. Knudsen, *Tägliche Rundschau*, Berlin, 14, V, 1917.

G. v. Lukács, *Frankfurter Zeitung*, 31, III, 1917.

G. F. Plotke, *Nord. u. Süd*, Breslau, Aprilheft, pp. 113–115 (1917).

P. Wüst, *Lit. Zentralblatt f. Deutschland*, Beilage, "Die schöne Literatur," pp. 225–230 (1917).

2. Erich Everth has expanded the appreciative attitude toward Meyer's style manifest in his twenty-page review, which rejects Baumgarten's results, into a delicate but

stimulating book entitled *Conrad Ferdinand Meyer, Dichtung und Persönlichkeit* (Dresden, 1924). Concerning himself neither with a critical examination of Meyer's problematical personality nor with an evaluation of his works, Everth, more interested "die Eigenart des Dichters aufzuspüren und zu verstehen, als ein examen rigorosum über den Grad seiner Begabung und seines Könnens abzuhalten," produces a careful and comprehending work, characterized by an over-refined and somewhat anaemic aestheticism that reminds one of the most coldly formal and bloodless phase of Meyer's own aristocratic reserve.

9 1. Br., II, 86.
2. *Deutsche Zeitschrift* (July and August, 1901).
10 1. Ge., 325–329.
2. Ge., 326–327.
3. Frey, 287.
4. Betsy Meyer, 163.
11 1. Br., II, 239; Korrodi, 50.
2. Br., I, 232.
3. *Ibid.*, in a letter to Rahn, January 18, 1872.
4. Frey, 225, 287.
5. Ge., 3.
6. Ge., 190.
12 1. "Die Gestalt, in der wir heute *Huttens letzte Tage* geniessen, ist nicht die ursprüngliche, sondern das Ergebnis unablässig zum Höchsten strebender Kunstübung. Bis in die allerletzten Jahre hat der Dichter an Stoff und Form seines Werkes gefeilt, und jede der zehn Auflagen, die er erlebte, sieht anders aus. So beträgt die Anzahl der Stücke in der ersten 54, in der vierten 76, in der letzten 71." — Maync, 127.
2. Frey, 245 ff.
3. Ge., on the unnumbered page between title-page and table of contents.
4. Korrodi, 55–56.
5. Frey, 287.
6. Br., II, 144.
13 1. Br., II, 207.
2. Br., II, 208. Cf. A. B., 244.

3. Br., II, 201, underscored.
4. Br., II, 202, in a postscript to the same letter of August 31, 1891.
5. Br., II, 202.
6. Br., II, 204.
7. Br., II, 204, footnote 1. "Bedenklich war, dass ihn Druckfehler wie ein wirkliches Unheil betrübten." — Frey, 356.
8. Baumgarten, 211.
9. Paul Wüst, *Gottfried Keller und C. F. Meyer in ihrem persönlichen und literarischen Verhältnis* (Leipzig, 1911).

14 1. Frey, *Albrecht Haller*, 89.
2. Frey, 286, 293.
3. February 28, 1824; also applied to Meyer by Moser, xv.

15 1. "Das sind seine eigenen Worte." — Frey, 293.
2. Ge., 4.
3. Br., II, 86.
4. Br., II, 306.
5. V., 199.
6. M., 92.
7. R., 333.
8. R., 272.
9. Ge., 161.

16 1. Betsy Meyer, 165, "Abschiedslied an Rom," 1864 (not incorporated in the collected poems). Frey, 126; Maync, 99.
2. Betsy Meyer, 162. Cf. Maync, 94.
3. Br., II, 222, and Frey, 308.
4. Communicated to Frey by Keller; cf. Frey, 307, 422.
5. Conveniently accessible in Wüst, 89.

17 1. Br., II, 137, letter of September 11, 1887.
2. "M. Angelo allerdings hat sich mit Hülfe seiner anatomischen Studien ein eignes Riesengeschlecht erschaffen." — Br., II, 223.
3. d'Harcourt, 304–305, and Moser, xxiv, make similar enumerations.
4. Schiller, *Sämtliche Werke*, Säkular-Ausgabe, XVI, 24. Meyer, in turning from his own time to great heroes of the past, is not unlike Karl Moor: "Mir ekelt vor diesem tintenklecksenden Säkulum, wenn ich in meinem Plutarch lese von grossen Menschen." — *Ibid.*, III, 16.

5. Frey, 134.

6. "Nicht unter 6000 Fuss Höhe darf unser heuriges Berg-quartier liegen. Ich bedarf Schneenähe. Die Herberge soll höchstens vier Gastzimmerchen haben, geländerlose Treppen und Bedienung ohne Kellner. Sie darf nur nach frischem Heu riechen." — Betsy Meyer, 189–190.

18 1. Frey, 318. He invites Lingg for a visit "in diesen *grossen* Räumen" (Br., II, 292). He comes back to these twelve-foot-high rooms of his new house again and again in his correspondence (Brw. Meyer-Rodenberg, 88; Brw. Meyer-François, 17, 21, 40, 119, 232). Of a former residence, *Seehof*, he wrote to Louis Vulliemin, April 26, 1868 (cf. Bibliothèque Universelle, November, December, 1899, Langmesser, 61–62, and d'Harcourt, 170), "C'est pour moi un véritable plaisir d'habiter une ancienne maison de campagne zurichoise; et surtout la hauteur des chambres (12 pieds) peu habituelle dans notre pays m'inspire les sentiments les plus élevés."

2. R., 344. Meyer says almost the same of himself: "Mein Auge bedarf zuweilen der Ebene, der Weite." — Brw. Meyer-François, 104.

3. To Kögel. Cf. d'Harcourt, 435.

4. "Es hängt ferner mit den Träumen von einer spezifisch schweizerischen Literatur zusammen, die ein baarer Unsinn sind." — Br., II, 26.

5. "Sie wissen, wie viel ich Deutschland, woher mir so viele Ermuthigungen, und stets zur rechten Stunde, gekommen sind, zu danken habe. Solches gelegentlich zu bezeugen hat mir stets Freude gemacht. Aber auch ganz abgesehen von meinem persönlichen Verhältnisse zur deutschen Literatur, habe ich die allgemeine Überzeugung, dass Zusammenhang und Anschluss an das grosse deutsche Leben für uns Schweizer etwas Selbstverständliches und Notwendiges ist. Ja, ich habe die Stärkung dieses Bedürfnisses stets als den genauen Gradmesser gründlicher Bildung betrachtet. Es ist, nach meiner Überzeugung, ein unermessliches Gut, dass wir, unbeschadet unserer Eigenthümlichkeit, einem weiten sprachlichen Gebiete und einer grossen nationalen Cultur angehören und uns nicht, wie etwa die Holländer, in einem engen particularen

Kreise bewegen." — Br., II, 389. Cf. also Br., I, 176, "Und die Deutschen (oder wir Deutsche) sollen unzweifelhaft ein grosses Volk werden!"
6. Brw. Meyer-Rodenberg, 89. Cf. Lerber, 146; Maync, 107.
7. Br., II, 168.
8. Linden, 46.
9. Everth, 222.
19 1. Brw. Meyer-François, 108.
2. *Ibid.*, 12.
3. Br., I, 138.
4. Wüst, 90, 182.
5. Br., I, 260. Cf. Everth, 235, "Viele Künstler aus Meyers Generation erstickten bei geschichtlichen Themen in archäologischem Kleinkram: Architekten, die aus Gelehrsamkeit Motive häuften, bis grosse Gelegenheiten verdorben und vertan waren, oder die Meininger, oder Piloty und Makart, von Alma Tadema zu schweigen."
6. L., 211.
7. "Dante für sein Theil lächelte zum ersten und einzigen Mal an diesem Abende." (M., 105).
20 1. Br., I, 160.
2. Köster, Storm-Keller Brw.², 171, 194.
3. R., 370–371. Cf. Everth, 30, 183, who there cites Meyer's phrases rather inaccurately.
4. M., 122.
5. M., 125–126.
6. M., 98.
7. R., 311.
8. L., 206.
21 1. L., 174.
2. M., 108.
3. Everth, 272.
4. M., 94–95; d'Harcourt, 517; Maync, 87.
5. A. B., 105–106.
6. To Kögel. Cf. d'Harcourt, 229, footnote 1.
7. In the unfinished fragment, *Ein Gewissensfall.* Langmesser, 474; d'Harcourt, 228, and *ibid.*, footnote 1; also Maync, 88–89.
22 1. Br., I, 138.
2. Br., I, 128.

3. Cf. Hans Bracher, *Rahmenerzählung und Verwandtes bei G. Keller, C. F. Meyer und Th. Storm*. Ein Beitrag zur Technik der Novelle (Leipzig [Haessel], 1924²).

4. Br., II, 340–341.

5. Brw. Meyer-François, 37.

23 1. *Ibid.*, 48. To Adolf Frey he wrote (Br., I, 340), "Der Hutten ist übrigens 'intimer' als alle meine Lyrica zusammen."

2. Ge., 183.

3. Ge., on the unnumbered page between title-page and table of contents.

4. "die lyrische Attitüde Meyers, die Attitüde des Dichters, der sich aus dem Gedicht zurückzieht." — Baumgarten, 208; *Ztft. f. Ä.*, VII, 388.

5. "Ich finde, ein Romanschreiber hat nicht das Recht seine Meinung über irgend etwas auszusprechen. Hat der liebe Gott sie je gesagt, seine Meinung?" This statement, cited by P. Witkop, *G. Keller als Lyriker* (1911), 13, might be applied to Meyer (Korrodi, 49; Faesi, 135), as also the words of Flaubert, "L'homme n'est rien, l'oeuvre est tout."

24 1. Ge., 335.

2. Frey, 298.

3. M., 129.

4. Ge., 25.

5. Ge., 335.

25 1. Sulger-Gebing, *C. F. Meyers Michelangelo-Gedichte*, Abhandlungen zur deutschen Literaturgeschichte, Franz Muncker dargebracht (München, 1916), 208–235; also *C. F. Meyers Gedichte aus dem Stoffgebiet der Antike in ihren Beziehungen zu Werken der bildenden Kunst*, Festschrift für Berthold Litzmann, hg. von Carl Enders (Bonn, 1920), 362–412; and especially "C. F. Meyers Werke in ihren Beziehungen zur bildenden Kunst," *Euphorion* (1921), Bd. 23, 422–495.

2. Ge., 25.

3. ". . . das fortwährende Zusammenleben mit den Meisterwerken der bildenden Künste mich mannigfach anregt." — Br., II, 227.

4. Frey, 307.

5. Br., I, 193.
6. P., 218.

26 1. Brw. Meyer-François, 54.
2. Kögel, 31. Cf. Wüst, 147.
3. "Der Gedichtband, den Meyer zuletzt herausgegeben
hat, gehört zu den Dutzend unserer Literatur, dessen
Aneignung für jede tiefere ästhetische Natur einfach
Pflicht ist; für alle ist er freilich nicht." — A. Bartels,
Geschichte d. d. Literatur (1909), II, 661.

27 1. Romance influences on the poetry and personality of
Meyer have been recently treated in connected form by
H. v. Lerber, *Der Einfluss der französischen Sprache und
Literatur auf C. F. Meyer und seine Dichtung* (Bern, 1924),
and K. E. Lusser, *C. F. Meyer. Das Problem seiner Jugend
unter besonderer Berücksichtigung der deutschen und romanischen Bildungseinflüsse* (Leipzig, 1926). Previous works
had touched on the problem; e. g., d'Harcourt, "Influence
générale de Mérimée et de la littérature française sur
Meyer," 298–299, 477, *et passim.* Cf., e. g., "A Rome
comme à Paris, Conrad est frappé par le symétrie, le sens
latin de l'ordonnance" (136). "Son oeuvre poétique . . .
a la royale froideur, l'incomparable ordonnance conven-
tionelle des jardins du grand siècle" (306). Also, to
mention only the earliest and latest of the German biog-
raphies, Frey, 79, 178; Maync, 99–104.
I touch on the problem later in this treatise and expect
to come back to it in a special article, *Romance and Germanic Traits in Conrad Ferdinand Meyer* and in a more
general work, *The German Sense of Form.*
2. The following chapters take up in detail former treatments of this problem by Baumgarten, Everth, Korrodi,
Linden, Lusser, *et al.*

28 1. Br., II, 86. Meyer to Hermann Haessel, June 16, 1879.

29 1. Cf. Everth, 16, "Aber von dialekthafter Färbung zeigt
er wenig Spuren"; Korrodi, 57, "Mit einem grossen Stil
konnte er Fremdwörter und zu modern anklingende
Wörter nicht mehr vereinbaren"; Wüst, 103, etc.
2. Cf. my article, "The Language of Conrad Ferdinand
Meyer's Lyric Poems," *JEGP*, XXX, No. 4 (October,
1931), 531–555.

3. E.g., Eppich (H., 83); Gau (R., 342); Hort (P., 241; R., 304; A. B., 75); Lenz (J. J., 234); Zähre (V., 149); glimmen (A., 197; M., 29; H., 100); klimmen (R., 305; A. B., 192), etc.

4. Ge., 253.

5. M., 47.

6. P., 218.

7. M., 98, "das Uebrige vergass ich."

8. R., 311, "sie hielt inne, um das reine Ohr Stemmas nicht zu beleidigen."

30 1. L., 206, "einen Viehkerl, wenn ich das Wort vor den Ohren der Majestät aussprechen darf."

2. L., 174, "niemals, auch nicht erzählungsweise, ein gemeines oder beschimpfendes, kurz ein unkönigliches Wort in den Mund zu nehmen."

3. Cf. Korrodi, 108, "Diese wählerische Renaissancegesinnung verrät seine Wortwahl, die das gewöhnliche Wort an das urbanere, ich möchte sagen, höfische Synonym eintauscht. . . . Nie wird ein Achill kleistisch sprechen: 'Sie schwitzen'; C. F. Meyers Helden schwitzen nie." It is interesting to note in this connection that one of Meyer's characters, an officer, criticizes his troops when they perspire and "nur darum weil er selbst nie schwitze" (L., 193).

4. Ge., 27. Cf. also for *wallen*: Ge., 15, 27, 141, 147, 152, 155, 166, 269, etc. There is, of course, good poetic precedent for *wallen*. Köster designates it as a *Modewort*, abhorred by Schönaich, and gives instances of its use (Köster, *Schönaich*, 401). Calvör finds it frequently in Wieland (Calvör, *Wieland*, 59).

5. Ge., 277.

6. E., 90.

7. Ge., 177.

8. Ge., 69.

9. Ge., 71. Cf. also for *wandeln*: Ge., 25, 33, 74, 92, 163, 215, 229, 238, 273, 275, 277; and V., 79, 103, 132; A. B., 39; Hu., 67, 113; J. J., 232, 261; M., 17, 49; H., 164, etc.

10. Ge., 46.

11. Ge., 230. Cf. also for *wandern*: Ge., 46, 47, 67, 77, 91, 93, 99, 112, 145, 160, 171, 200, 201, 231, 293, 302, 396, 397; Hu., 8, 143, etc.

12. L., 242. Cf. also for *schleichen*: Ge., 104, 125, 130, 187, 196, 265, 275, 329, 336, 371, 390; Hu., 57, 138; E., 69; P., 260, etc.

13. Ge., 105. Cf. also for *pilgern*: Ge., 89, 105, 127; Hu., 94, etc.

14. Ge., 328. Cf. also for *irren*: Ge., 21, 51, 108, 109, 124, 172, 268; G., 351; Hu., 24, etc.

31 1. Ge., 143.

2. Ge., 353.

3. Ge., 223.

4. Ge., 316.

5. Ge., 71. H. H. Stevens, *Description in Grillparzer*, etc. (H. U. Diss., unprinted [1916], 233–234), cites a similar use in Grillparzer. Medea is described, "*Die* aber ward gesehn/Den goldnen Schmuck um ihre Schultern tragend/ Zur selben Stunde *schreitend* durch die Nacht."

6. V., 185.

7. V., 205.

8. *schreiten*: Ge., 15, 35, 66, 74, 79, 89, 91, 95, 105, 113, 116, 121, 124, 130, 145, 154, 161, 162, 176, 190, 200, 201, 202, 210, 215, 223, 230, 231, 250, 261, 275, 292, 316, 326, 343, 353, 380, 392, 400, etc., etc.; Hu., 27, 72, 120, 134, 143, 161; E., 7, 52, 57; V., 15, 79; M., 19, 107, 115; J. J., 271; S., 122; G., 340; P., 232, 245, 262, 263, 264; R., 381, etc.

9. E., 27; R., 381, "auf stillen Sohlen nachschreiten."

10. L., 223.

11. Ge., 396.

12. Ge., 161.

32 1. J. J., 259.

2. Ge., 145.

3. Ge., 350. In Titian Meyer finds "grosse Geberde (z. B. beim Schreiten)." —Br., II, 222.

4. Ge., 252.

5. *lauschen*: Ge., 18, 19, 52, 82, 89, 101, 106, 110, 129, 190, 192, 221, 226, 229, 234, 237, 250, 253, 265, 271, 276, 286,

290, 305, 309, 312, 317, 336, 354, 396, etc.; Hu., 13, 39, 42, 93, 132; E., 8, 18, 32, 36, 103.

6. *lauschen:* V., 62, 67, 97, 104, 165; R., 324; H., 27, 111, 214; J. J., 19, 27, 29, 48, 127; P., 217, 262; M., 99, 120; G., 293; A., 94; L., 179; S., 187, 207, etc.

7. V., 41.

8. Hu., 38. Cf. also for *lugen:* Ge., 371, etc.

9. Ge., 265. Cf. also for *spähen:* Ge., 21, 29, 53, 265, 301, etc.; Hu., 28, 149; E., 37; R., 391; L., 179.

10. Ge., 90. Cf. also for *weisen:* E., 61; Hu., 144; V., 27; L., 251; P., 242; G., 294; A. B., 65; R., 310, 342, 400, etc.

33 1. Ge., 85.

2. Ge., 24. Cf. also for *lechzen:* Ge., 24, 85, 114, 261, 346, 380, etc.; R., 287, etc. *darben:* Ge., 24, 34, 65, 162, 207, 256, 341, 373, etc.; J. J., 139; V., 102, etc.

3. Ge., 35. Cf. also for *nippen:* Ge., 35, 221, 229, etc.; J. J., 4, 21, etc.

4. Ge., 85. Cf. also for *schlürfen:* Ge., 3, 85, 96, 114, 123, 162, 233, 234, 277, 380, 386, etc.; Hu., 7, 14; E., 36; A. B., 30, 56; V., 208; H., 9, 207; J. J., 4, 19; A., 72; R., 364; M., 145; S., 137, etc.

5. Ge., 114.

6. M., 71.

7. V., 167.

8. Ge., 346.

9. *seufzen:* Ge., 271, 329, 384, etc.; V., 132; A., 77; M., 10, 37; G., 277; P., 218; R., 403; L., 207; A. B., 44, 135, etc.

10. *keuchen:* Ge., 55, 98, 346, etc.; Hu., 152; E., 81; V., 165, 186; R., 287, 398, etc.

11. *stöhnen:* Ge., 19, 21, 121, 279, 305, 335, 375, 381, etc.; Hu., 24, 104, 164; P., 252; H., 217; V., 70, 210, 215; S., 101, 179; R., 231, 376; M., 31, 100, 150; L., 221; A. B., 93, etc.

12. V., 23, 89, 116, 217; P., 230; H., 62, 156; R., 275, 388; G., 320; L., 202, etc.

13. A. B., 196.

34 1. Ge., 26.

2. Ge., 13.

3. Ge., 379.

4. Ge., 380. Korrodi (105) writes, "Der grosse Stil hat ihn zum Eklektiker und Gourmand gemacht," when he doubtless means to have written *Gourmet*.

5. *Becher:* Ge., 198, 221, 233, 236, 264, etc.

6. *Kelch:* Ge., 179, etc. "Aus den *Kelchen* schütten wir die Neigen."

7. *Pokal:* Ge., 386, etc.

8. H., 176.

9. Ge., 162.

10. Ge., 203.

11. P., 268. Cf. also for *Schale*: Ge., 51, 155, 162, 203, 204, 221, 233, 256, etc.; H., 83, 207; J. J., 7, 292; V., 121; R., 293, 397, etc.

12. J. J., 77.

35   1. V., 168.

2. V., 17.

3. H., 72.

4. Ge., 354.

5. "Just zwischen Tageslicht und Ampelschein" (Hu., 160).

6. *Ampel:* Ge., 14, 111, 190, 205, 255, 263, 348, 354, 396; Hu., 160; E., 23, etc.

7. *Ampel:* J. J., 31; A. B., 186; H., 91, 111; V., 72, 152, 183, etc.

8. E., 23.

9. Ge., 190. A related interest in careful arrangement of light and shade may make *das Halbdunkel* such a favorite setting for his stories; *Halbdunkel:* P., 246, 260; A. B., 89, 140, 197; S., 135; G., 300; M., 1, 6, 8, 105, 162; R., 355; V., 121, etc.

10. Ge., 391.

11. Ge., 98. Cf. also for *Pfühl:* Ge., 62, 98, 249, 381, 394, etc.; Hu., 123; H., 87; V., 169; P., 243, etc.

12. V., 169.

13. Ge., 62.

14. R., 348.

15. V., 205. Cf. also for *Mantel*: Ge., 5, 18, 126, 146, 265, 312, 313, 354, 359, 400, etc.; Hu., 127; E., 6; H., 1, 59, 75, 172; A., 53; R., 355, 400, 402; M., 3, 51, 82; V.,

10, 205; S., 183, 186; J. J., 4, 27, 139, 241; G., 307, 311, 316, etc.

16. Ge., 312. Cf. the title, "Der gleitende Purpur."
17. Ge., 319.

36 1. Ge., 284.
2. R., 381.
3. R., 319; A. B., 163.
4. V., 124.
5. P., 245.
6. Cf. also for *Sohlen*: Ge., 206, 277; H., 193; M., 66, 107; A. B., 155, 163; V., 64, 124; E., 17, 35, 80, 90; R., 310, 317, 319, 381, etc.
7. Ge., 277.
8. E., 90.
9. *Ross*: Ge., 64, 159, 176, etc.; M., 24; R., 371, 378, etc.
10. *Gaul*: H., 2, 74; M., 47, etc.
11. Ge., 392.
12. A. B., 1, 14. Cf. also for *Zelter*: H., 40, 72, etc. There is manifest also in the substitutions for *Pferd* Meyer's use of the specific word for the general, which I discuss in detail later, and his use of the horse as a method of characterization. Angela Borgia and the somewhat effeminate Thomas Becket, for example, may well be seated on a palfrey, a woman's horse.
13. Ge., 319.
14. V., 202–203.

37 1. *Sänfte*: Ge., 251, 287, 319, 342, etc.; J. J., 205; A. B., 97, 190; V., 43, 56, 64, 202; M., 16, 82, 101, 122, 134, etc.
2. *Barke*: Ge., 68, 139, 203, etc.; M., 12, etc.
3. *Ferge*: Ge., 19; Hu., 114, "Der kleine Ferge." Title: Hu., 114; M., 13, etc.
4. *Ringelhaar*: Ge., 290; Hu., 41, etc.
5. *Kraushaar*: A. B., 142; V., 18; M., 18; G., 336; P., 224, 267, etc. Cf. also *Lockenkopf*: A., 70; *Flachskopf*: G., 339, etc.
6. G., 339.
7. Ge., 317, 319.
8. Ge., 46. Cf. also for *Locken*, etc.: Ge., 11, 46, 128, 133, 144, 146, 153, 177, 232, 283, 287, 293, 392.

9. *greis:* Ge., 73, 85, 111, 146, 221, 231, 255, 328, 351, etc.; P., 217, etc. Cf. the noun, *der Greis:* Ge., 102, 111; P., 218, 219; Hu., 138, etc.
10. *siech:* Ge., 286; Hu., 44, 131, 159, etc.
11. Hu., 44.
12. V., 81.
13. Ge., 34.
14. J. J., 114.
15. Ge., 168.
16. V., 205. Cf. also G., 311, 314.

38 1. J. J., 209.
2. J. J., 274.
3. J. J., 299.
4. J. J., 330.
5. *roth:* Ge., 7, 47, 52, 55, 71, 72, 103, 132, 152, 194, 198, 202, 212, 269, 308, 317, 367, 380, etc.; V., 94, 205; M., 94; L., 204; R., 363; J. J., 7, 209, 274, 299, 330, etc.
6. Cf. *Ztft. f. Ä.,* IV, 565, footnote 2.
7. *purpur:* Ge., 39, 72, 81, 118, 125, 133, 145, 149, 168, 171, 216, 227, 269, 284, 312, 314, 319, etc.
8. *golden:* Ge., 4, 21, 34, 64, 66, 78, 96, 129, 143, 198, 233, 239, 298, 315, 346, 377, 392, etc.; Pescara lies "auf dem goldenen Bette des Thronhimmels" (V., 222). In some of these cases "golden" is used merely as a "poetic" word.
9. *blond:* Ge., 17, 48, 80, 106, 107, 146, 147, 150, 210, 224, 226, 287, 292, 296, 300, 315, 323, 347, 398, etc.; G., 304; V., 180; L., 190, 237; M., 23, 24, 55, etc.
10. Ge., 144.
11. Ge., 242.
12. Cf. M. L. Taylor, *A Study of the Technique in K. F. Meyer's Novellen* (Diss. [Chicago, 1909], 13 ff.)
13. Ge., 210.
14. Ge., 226.
15. J. J., 209.
16. J. J., 274.
17. *blau:* Ge., 26, 41, 56, 59, 60, 81, 95, 102, 108, 109, 117, 123, 126, 131, 135, 139, 143, 147, 161, 184, 213, 233, 273, 286, 287, 293, 303, 345, etc.; L., 218; H., 227; P., 237; A., 33, 38, 78; V., 46, 126, 180; S., 189; Hu., 51, etc. Cf. also *blauen* (Umblauen): Ge., 43, 44, 93, 96, 143, 144,

241, 256, 295, etc., and *Blau*: Ge., 10, 28, 48, 49, 123, 211, 243, 251, 329, 369, etc.

18. S., 189.
19. Hu., 51.
39 1. *fahl*: Ge., 10, 348, 389, etc.; H., 90; V., 86; G., 308; S., 147; J. J., 221; M., 45, 164, etc.; *falb*: Ge., 132, 241, etc.; J. J., 331, etc.

2. L. Franck, *Statistische Untersuchungen über die Verwendung der Farben in den Dichtungen Goethes* (Giessen, 1909); Karl u. Marie Groos, "Die optischen Qualitäten in der Lyrik Schillers," *Ztft. f. Ä.* (1909), 559 ff.; Karl Groos, u. Ilse Netto u. Marie Groos, "Die Sinnesdaten im 'Ring des Nibelungen,'" *Archiv f. d. G. Psy.*, XXII, 4, 461 ff.; K. Groos and I. Netto, *Über die visuellen Sinneseindrücke in Shakespeares lyrischen Dichtungen*, Eng. Stud. (1911), 43, 27 ff.; E. Thorstenberg, *Lessing's Appreciation of Color as an Element of Effect in Poetry* (Yale Diss., 1904); A. Gubelmann, *Studies in the Lyric Poems of Hebbel.* The sensuous in Hebbel's lyric poetry, N. H., 1912; V. D. Scudder, "The Prometheus Unbound of Shelley III," *Atlantic Monthly*, LXX, No. 419 (September, 1892), 394 ff.; Haberl Munrad, *Die Entwicklung des optischen und akustischen Sinns bei Shakespeare* (Berlin, 1913 [Dissertation Munich]); Müller-Gschwend, G. *Keller als lyrischer Dichter*, Berlin, 10 *Acta Germanica*, VII, 2, Über Kellers Koloristik, 191 ff.; Minna Jacobson, *Die Farben in der mhd. Dichtung der Blütezeit* (Leipzig, 1915), Teutonia, 22, etc.

3. Gubelmann, 79, for *red* in Hebbel; *ibid.*, 119 ff.
4. *braun*: Ge., 63, 96, 112, 132, 133, 150, 169, 172, 195, 229, 265, 293, 391, 401, etc.; V., 126; J. J., 14, 41, 119, etc.
5. *grün*: Ge., 22, 24, 29, 47, 56, 74, 89, 94, 98, 104, 116, 128, 139, 142, 194, 210, 340, 350, etc.; H., 65, etc. Cf. *grün* in Wilhelm Müller: "No color scheme could be more direct than Müller's. *Green* is his favorite hue, and in his songs of the road, particularly, he looks on nature through beryl-glasses."—P. Allen, *W. Müller and the German Volkslied* (Chicago, 1901), 136.
6. *schwarz*: Ge., 62, 94, 101, 143, 185, 242, 245, 251, 288, 311, 316, 317, etc.

7. *weiss:* Ge., 7, 19, 145, 154, 169, 230, 233, 244, 251, 293, 317, 389, etc.
8. *grau:* Ge., 91, 97, 124, 238, 256, etc. Cf. "den Felsen umschleichst du grau auf dem Grau." (Ge., 123.)
9. *gelb:* H., 64, 74; V., 179; S., 121.
10. *violett:* S., 152; H., 72.
11. Ge., 174.

40 1. Ge., 333.
2. Ge., 299.
3. V., 125.
4. H., 160.
5. *Die Rechte:* Ge., 18, 58, 114, 145, 226, 242, 264, 286, 298, 299, 329, 333, 347, etc.; Hu., 79, 132; V., 72, 186; R., 340; M., 55; S., 87; H., 109, 144, 146, 160; J. J., 49, 81, 299, etc.
6. *Die Linke:* Ge., 114, 145, 299, 333, etc.; V., 125; H., 109, 160, etc.
7. Korrodi, 116–119.
8. R., 285.
9. R., 325.
10. R., 373.
11. P., 234.
12. V., 127.
13. A. B., 173.
14. V., 74.
15. H., 194.

41 1. A. B., 79.
2. H., 136.
3. A. B., 233.
4. A. B., 141.
5. V., 115.
6. Diana in *Die Hochzeit des Mönchs.* Cf. Korrodi, 117: "Dieses schwere trochäische Relativgefüge ist nur die absichtlich prolongierte Vorbereitung für ihre Attribute, die sie herausmeisseln will."
7. V., 79, close of chapter ii.
8. Cf. "*Schelm* Graciosus" (R., 282).
9. Meyer to Rodenberg, March 19, 1884, Brw. Meyer-Rodenberg, 189. Cf. Langmesser, 135; Korrodi, 115; Everth, 44.

10. L. E., XXIV, 23 (September 1, 1922), 1413.
11. Korrodi, 113.
12. M., 121.

42 1. Ge., 116.
2. *frisch:* Ge., 16, 39, 49, 50, 70, 91, 129, 271, 273, 307, 313, 317, 324, 357, 365, 367, 371.
jung: Ge., 12, 15, 17, 27, 39, 40, 49, 50, 74, 75, 77, 85, 93, 122, 128, 140, 141, 147, 148, 161, 166, 175, 187, 191, 193, 200, 202, 221, 240, 248, 271, 276, 279, 288, 289, 290, 295, 296, 301, 306, 307, 308, 322, 324, 326, 328, 330, 357, 377, 396.
schön: Ge., 13, 21, 42, 144, 153, 157, 162, 234, 238, 271, 299, 307, 377.
süss: Ge., 6, 13, 62, 73, 75, 101, 113, 121, 154, 195, 197, 200, 203, 275, 290, 295, 296, 352, 357, 358, 359.
tief: Ge., 4, 8, 9, 68, 69, 94, 122, 125, 127, 163, 192, 263, 299.
voll: Ge., 3, 17, 45, 48, 64, 72, 85, 91, 107, 156, 169, 192, 203, 204, 221, 256, 326, 340, 358, 365, 382.
warm: Ge., 4, 10, 43, 166, 192, 213, 266, 276, 280, 299, 312, 316, 373, 375, 379.
weit: Ge., 5, 34, 90, 159, 166, 168, 230, 259, 330, 389.
3. Ge., 107.
4. Ge., 64.
5. Ge., 168.
6. *frech:* Ge., 55, 73, 259, 296, 308, 397; Hu., 77, 107, 279; G., 316; J. J., 93; L., 211; R., 274, 336, 373, 388; A. B., 19, 35; V., 12, 84, 88, 103, 114, 130, etc.
7. Hu., 77.
8. R., 388.
9. M., 160.
10. *wild:* Ge., 10, 14, 15, 18, 23, 73, 81, 83, 96, 100, 101, 108, 114, 128, 130, 131, 142, 168, 200, 204, 242, 255, 259, 264, 295, 297, 302, 308, 323, 341.
11. Ge., 200.

43 1. Mirabelle Miramion (L., 226).
2. L., 225.
3. L., 219.
4. "der sparsame Gebrauch der Epitheta bei Meyer." — Weise, *Aesthetik d. d. Sprache,* 199.

5. "Oft schwankte er zwischen einem halben Dutzend bezeichnenden Eigenschaftswörtern, von denen er eines nach dem andern wieder strich, ehe er zur endgültigen Wahl gelangte" (Frey, 281). Similarly Korrodi shows how carefully Meyer weighs the value of the epithet in his prose and suggests, "Die Gedichte zeigen vielleicht noch deutlicher diese feine Ueberlegungen über die Valeurs des Beiwortes" (Korrodi, 55, 115).

6. "The definition of good prose is — proper words in their proper places: of good verse — the most proper words in their proper places." — Coleridge, Table Talk, 1833.

7. Cf. the theory of "le mot propre," "le mot significatif," of Flaubert, who wrote, "Je veux trouver quatre ou cinq phrases que je cherche depuis bientôt un mois." Cf. Madame Bovary (Paris, 1910), 488, and also the introduction of Guy de Maupassant to the Oeuvres complètes de Flaubert (Paris, 1910).

8. R. M. Meyer (Stilistik, 50, footnote 6) cites Villers on Fr. Th. Vischer: "Kein Substantiv getraut sich auf die Strasse ohne die Begleitung von einem halben Dutzend Adjektivtrabanten."

9. Cf. the enumeration of these in my article on "The Language of Conrad Ferdinand Meyer's Lyric Poems," JEGP, XXX, No. 4 (October, 1931), 542–543.

10. Cf. my article on "The Language of Detlev von Liliencron's Lyrics and Ballads," JEGP, XXX, No. 2 (April, 1931), 236–254.

11. Cf. JEGP, XXX, No. 4 (October, 1931), 531–555.

44 1. glüh: Ge., 81, 271, 282.
harsch: Ge., 369, 400.
licht: Ge., 12, 34, 40, 78, 108, 131, 175.
schlemm: Ge., 294.
schrill: Ge., 170, 173.
schwank: E., 51; Hu., 52, 125, 140; M., 95.
wank: Ge., 105; E., 105.

2. "Kein Wunder dass die Partizipien des Präsens in der poetischen Sprache oft geradezu gehäuft werden. So verwendet Klopstock in der kurzen Ode über den Lehrling der Griechen deren 11, Schiller in den 100 Distischen seines 'Spaziergangs' 66." — Weise, Ä. d. d. S., 194.

3. Ge., 392.   Cf. also, G. 289–290.
4. Korrodi, 143.
5. Ge., 237.
45   1. Ge., 198.
2. Ge., 256.
3. Ge., 143.   Cf. also Ge., 132, 143, 156, 161, 224, 225, 226,
233, 235, 236, 237, 242, 244, 249, 256, 268, 369, etc.
4. Ge., 159.
5. Cf. *JEGP*, XXX, No. 4 (October, 1931), 548–549.
6. *ewig:* Ge., 4, 16, 46, 49, 69, 77, 86, 114, 140, 146, 169, 177,
259, 368, 397, 401.
7. *gewaltig:* Ge., 234, 245, 255, 261, 354, 359.
8. *heilig:* Ge., 66, 86, 117, 144, 166, 222, 259, 260, 280, 320,
346.
9. *mächtig:* Ge., 49, 105, 152, 160, 162, 245, 249, 255, 338,
371.
10. *nervig:* Ge., 163, 226, 335, 345, 354.
11. Ge., 159.
12. Ge., 390.
13. Ge., 160.
14. Ge., 335.
15. Ge., 354.
16. Ge., 154.
17. Ge., 221.
18. Ge., 396.
19. Ge., 381.
20. Ge., 159.
21. Ge., 236, 267.
22. Ge., 230, 256.
23. Ge., 193.
24. Ge., 389.
25. Ge., 252, 255.
26. Ge., 144.
27. Ge., 350.
46   1. *ekel:* Ge., 328, 373.
2. *frevel:* Ge., 61, 64, 149, 250, 298, 343, 394.
3. *grausam:* Ge., 14, 19, 24, 225.
4. *lüstern:* Ge., 19, 96, 252, 308.
5. A. B., 173.
6. J. J., 93.

7. Ge., 19.
8. Korrodi, 113.
9. A., 38.
10. Weise (*Ä. d. d. S.*, 196–197) gives such lists.
11. Paul Knauth, *Goethes Sprache und Stil im Alter* (Leipzig, 1898), 67.
12. E.g., Kleist, Minde-Pouet, 206 ff.; Grillparzer, Stevens, 232; Schiller, Wunderlich, 206; ("frei" is, for example, very frequent with Schiller); Klinger, Philipp, 22, etc. Cf. Marlowe's "black," Shelley's "light."
13. Korrodi, 114.
14. *rein:* Ge., 4, 18, 54, 69, 79, 89, 93, 96, 98, 154, 200, 230, 231, 232, 237, 310, 326, 354, 364, 379.
15. *keusch:* Ge., 18, 55, 132, 161, 196, 266, 326.
16. *kühl:* Ge., 10, 55, 91, 96, 124, 203, 210, 272, 275, 276, 317, 380.
17. *scheu:* Ge., 15, 82, 125, 145, 198, 227, 276, 329, 389, 400.
18. *schlank:* Ge., 18, 22, 31, 49, 59, 81, 91, 150, 159, 179, 190, 200, 203, 207, 230, 233, 238, 266, 276, 287, 307, 319, 327, 383, 384, 396.
19. *zart:* Ge., 6, 25, 34, 53, 74, 94, 151, 158, 187, 190, 195, 196, 198, 201, 204, 263, 266, 277, 307, 309, 317.

47   1. *blank:* Ge., 19, 63, 73, 97, 143, 229, 304, 308, 317, 319, 365.
2. *blass:* Ge., 16, 158, 185, 292, 380.
3. *bleich:* Ge., 57, 122, 145, 148, 160, 199, 204, 209, 218, 239, 241, 245, 286, 296, 308, 351, 371, 377, 379, 396.
4. *dunkel:* Ge., 24, 40, 43, 52, 70, 101, 134, 149, 161, 189, 206, 227, 229, 242, 249, 250, 265, 267, 304.
5. *düster:* Ge., 231, 272, 379, 381.
6. *hell:* Ge., 17, 21, 36, 37, 40, 47, 53, 54, 69, 74, 91, 96, 123, 153, 178, 214, 224, 230, 233, 242, 251, 260, 270, 290, 305, 307, 309, 330, 345, 370, 376, 377.
7. *licht:* Ge., 12, 34, 40, 78, 108, 131, 175.
8. *dumpf:* Ge., 3, 8, 9, 43, 52, 54, 59, 79, 81, 95, 101, 103, 122, 129, 145, 160, 167, 187, 227, 230, 246, 292, 363.
9. *leis:* Ge., 6, 36, 53, 68, 80, 98, 106, 117, 130, 188, 196, 207, 214, 215, 275, 290, 295, 329, 401.
10. *sacht:* Ge., 15, 18, 25, 41, 73, 89, 132, 133, 134, 187, 255.
11. *still:* Ge., 15, 16, 18, 40, 46, 68, 69, 73, 81, 83, 91, 93, 102,

107, 112, 119, 190, 196, 198, 205, 207, 230, 245, 248, 263, 272, 316, 328, 329, 401.

12. *Italienische Reise*, January 22, 1787, Jubiläumsausgabe 26, 191.

13. G. L. Kittredge, *Shakspere, an Address* (Cambridge, 1916), 49.

14. R. L. Stevenson, *Technical Elements of Style in Literature*, "Contents of the Phrase," Section 4, Biog. ed. (N. Y., 1905).

15. Ge., 227.

16. Ge., 262.

17. M., 38.

18. A. B., 198.

19. Hu., 99.

20. *dröhnen:* Ge., 79, 103, 162, 164, 167, 229, 242, 246, 260, 265, 295, 329, 390.
    gellen: Ge., 144, 162, 242, 252, 297, 359, 396.
    lodern: Ge., 4, 11, 76, 118, 133, 144, 168, 202, 238.
    lohen: Ge., 251, 263, 296.
    peitschen: Ge., 64, 231, 242, 304.
    quellen: Ge., 11, 50, 52, 252, 271, 327.
    zucken: Ge., 11, 55, 208, 262, 322.
    Similarly in the prose for all these verbs; e.g., *zucken:* V., 101; R., 304; A., 73; V., 35; M., 108, 145; A. B., 74, 173; L., 177, 183, 257, 266, etc.

48 1. Müller-Freienfels, *Poetik*, 82.

2. Brw. Meyer-François, 76.

3. "Es wäre möglich, dass mein Ohr feiner ist für das Französische als das Deutsche, geschulter jedenfalls." — Br., II, 164.

4. V., 118.

5. Müller-Gschwend, *G. K. als lyr. D.* (Berlin, 1910), 183.

49 1. *Rheinlande*, October, 1900.

2. Kalischer, 203.

3. Korrodi, 142. Cf. *ibid.*, 122 ff., 136 ff.

4. G. R. M. (1913), 306. Cf. also 440.

5. D. L. Z. (1913); M. 30, Sp. 1885.

6. Müller-Freienfels, *Psychologie der Kunst* (Leipzig, 1912), 71.

7. M. Dessoir, "Anschauung und Beschreibung," *Archiv f. syst. Phil.*, X, 48.
8. Woldemar Masing, "Sprachliche Musik in Goethes Lyrik," *Q. u. F.* (1910), 108. Cf. also Marcelle Faessler, *Untersuchungen zum Prosa-Rhythmus in C. F. Meyers Novellen*, Sprache und Dichtung, Heft 32 (Bern, 1925).
9. Robert Chenault Givler spends eight years in psychological laboratories, "in which years 18,000 lines of poetry were phonetically measured and tabulated, involving the enumeration of nearly 540,000 sounds; the measurement of the records obtained in the laboratory involved nearly 300,000 bits of data; the occupation of the mean, the mean variation and its range for all the experiments and the making of the rank lists brings the total number of computations to more than a million" (641–642), in an effort to determine the emotional effect of the speech element in poetry by the process of transmogrification, that is, transmogrifying "poems into lines having the same sounds as the original poems but possessing no logical, rhetorical or verbal meaning" (212). This work culminates in the results he brings forward in a six-hundred-page dissertation, *The Psychophysical Effect of the Elements of Speech in Relation to Poetry*, H. U. Diss. (unprinted, 1914).

50 1. Givler, 3.
2. Ge., 113.
3. Ge., 144. The whole poem repays investigation from this point of view.
4. Ge., 42. Cf. d'Harcourt, 303.
5. Ge., 302.
6. Moser, xlii.
7. Ge., 72.

51 1. Moser, xciv.
2. Saitschik, 268.
3. All critics have speculated on Meyer's failure to produce drama. Cf. Baumgarten, 163; Everth, 145; d'Harcourt, 522; Linden, 152; Maync, 322; and on the whole subject Hans Corrodi, *C. F. Meyer und sein Verhältnis zum Drama* (Leipzig [Haessel], 1923).
4. R. u. B., 61. Cf. Moser, lxvii.
5. Ge., 349.

52 1. Wüst, G. R. M. (1913), 442.
2. Moser, lxiv ff., esp. lxvi.
3. Moser, ii, 83.
4. Ge., 383.
5. Ge., 355.
6. Ge., 143.
7. Ge., 64.
53 1. Ge., 381.
2. Ge., 292.
3. Ge., 227.
4. Ge., 226.
54 1. Ge., 335.
2. Bächthold, *Keller*, III, 547.
55 1. Storm-Keller Briefe, ed. Köster, 143.
2. *edel:* Ge., 39, 73, 80, 90, 91, 111, 146, 150, 161, 190, 233, 244, 248, 264, 311, 333, 338, 372, 387; Hu., 5, 37, 109, 151, 166; M., 41, 146; J. J., 150, 256; A. B., 14, 16, 20, 111, 217.
3. *erhaben:* Ge., 234, 269, 397, etc.
4. *üppig:* Ge., 6, 85, 119, 140, 142, 159, 326, 385; Hu., 64; A. B., 33; S., 177; P., 219; H., 36, 83; J. J., 39, 56, 180, 273.
5. D. L. Z. (1913) M. 30, Sp. 1885.
6. C. Busse, *Tägliche Rundschau*, October 26, 27, 1908. Cf. d'Harcourt, 303.
7. Liliencron, *Werke* (Berlin, 1913⁴), II, 211.
8. d'Harcourt, 438.
9. F. Th. Vischer to Meyer, December 13, 1886 (Br., II, 178). Cf. d'Harcourt, 458.
56 1. Kalischer, 11.
2. Korrodi, 63.
3. Linden, 144.
4. Br., I, 447.
5. J. J., 86.
6. L., 176.
7. S., 200.
8. G., 295–296.
57 1. Moser, xliii.
2. Moser, lxvii. "Die Erzählung aus Plutarch *Der neue Name* oder (lxviii) *Thespesius* ist in den *Balladen* noch in 25 vierzeiligen Strophen breitgelegt, 1875 (II, 66 ff.) sind

es deren noch 16, und heute umfasst sie 34 Iambenzeilen. *Himmelsnähe* bestand ehedem aus neun Vierzeilern, ging dann auf fünf und zuletzt auf vier herab; *Michel Angelos Gebet* ist im Laufe der Zeit um sieben Strophen verengt worden. Das kleine achtzeilige Lied *Neujahrsglocken* (II, 13 f.) hat sich offenbar aus dem grösseren fünfstrophigen *Der Glocken Rede* herausgeschält; *Schlacht der Bäume* enthält heute noch vier statt neun Strophen; *Der Zweikampf* ist gar von 23 vierzeiligen Strophen (Ball. S. 33) auf sechs Distichen zusammengeschmolzen. Die Ballade *Das Auge des Blinden* (*Don Juan de Austria*) hatte ursprünglich 31, später (II, 48) 21 Strophen, und heute sind es deren noch 13. Zahlreiche andre Gedichte erhielten eine mehr oder minder wesentliche Kürzung." Cf. Korrodi, 54, 60.

3. Cf. *JEGP*, XXX, No. 4 (October, 1931), 547–548.

4. "Held, du *zürntest, schlummertest* du nicht " (Ge., 159); "Was *frommt'* es, *trüg'* ich hären Kleid/ Und *mangelte* der Liebe" (Ge., 318). These tenses are also more elevated: in poetry, "Von deinem Tische *stiessest* du den Zecher,/*Entrissest* ihm den eisgewürzten Becher,/Und *rolltest* ihn hohnlachend durch die Klüfte" (Ge., 121); "Du selbst *verlorest'*s im Gedräng der Schlacht!" (Ge., 248), as in prose: "*Kämest* du heim, ich *bäte* dich" (R., 290).

5. Korrodi, 119. Similarly, Kalischer, 194.

6. P., 266.

7. R., 355.

8. M., 48–49.

9. "Dann wisperte er Victorien ins Ohr, 'Morone, Buffone.'" (V., 51.)

10. Korrodi, 96, 97.

11. M., 56.

12. A. B., 84.

13. V., 25.

14. A. B., 91.

58 1. Hu., 31.

2. Ge., 231.

3. Ge., 382.

4. Ge., 282.

59 1. M., 165.
    2. V., 161.
    3. V., 212.
    4. M., 121.
    5. Ge., 249.
    6. Ge., 229.
    7. Ge., 19.
    8. Ge., 143.
    9. Hu., 86.
   10. Ge., 249.
   11. Ge., 397.
   12. Ge., 55.

60 1. Ge., 254.
    2. Ge., 250. Cf. Moser, xciii, "Ein gedankenschleudernder
       Achill, fixiert er alsdann eine Bilderreihe mit Substan-
       tiven, die wie Male dastehen. Durch eine einzige Zeile
       jagt er eine ganze zusammenhängende Folge von Er-
       scheinungen an unserm Auge vorbei."
    3. Karl Henckell, *Deutsche Dichter seit Heine*, 68.
    4. H. Friedrichs, *Deutsche Zeitschrift* (July, August, 1901).

61 1. R. u. B., 91. Cf. Moser, lxvii.
    2. Ge., 254.
    3. Ge., 236.

62 1. R., 373–374.
    2. R., 370.
    3. Ge., 224.

63 1. Ge., 250.
    2. R. u. B., 54. Cf. Moser, xciii.
    3. Schopenhauer, *Werke*, ed. Grisebach, Reclam V, 555.

64 1. Schlegel, *Vorlesungen*, D. L. D., XVII, 293.
    2. Spiero, *Liliencron*, 138.
    3. C. Weise, *Curiöse Gedanken*, ed. 1693, 185–186.
    4. *Ibid.*, 182.
    5. Cf. Trog, 142; Moser, xciii, "Er spricht in Ellipsen,
       später bis zur Manieriertheit."
    6. Ge., 385.
    7. Cf. my "Comparison of the Poetry of Liliencron and
       Meyer," to appear in the *JEGP*, April, 1932.

8. Kraeger, 360. *Atlantic Monthly*, CXVIII, No. 3 (September, 1916), 432, and on the whole matter cf. *supra*, footnote 7.

9. "Ebenso erklärte er, seiner Neigung zur Kürze, zu allzustarker Verdichtung und epigrammatischer Knappheit entgegenarbeiten zu wollen, welche sonst leicht mit den Jahren überhandnehmen könnte, und freute sich, gegen frühere Erzählungen eine grössere Breite und Fülle gewonnen zu haben." — Maync, 277. Cf. Brw. Meyer-Rodenberg, 226–227, 238, 242.

65 1. M., 90.

66 1. Meyer to Hermann Friedrichs, 1890, *Deutsche Zeitschrift* (July, 1901), cited by d'Harcourt, 504–505.

2. Betsy Meyer, 161, 163. Cf. d'Harcourt, 211.

67 1. "Nun sind es aber neben der Kompression gerade die Reinheit und Prägnanz des Gedankens, auf die Meyer mit jeder Umwandlung immer mehr abzielt." — Moser, lxxx.

2. Moser ii, 21.

3. Ge., 13.

4. "Der Genius, der die Fackel einfach 'senkt,' könnte sie auch wieder heben und das Leben neu triumphieren lassen; der sie aber 'löscht'; das ist unzweifelhaft der Tod." — Moser, xxxvi.

5. Ge., 371. Cf. Moser, xl.

6. Ge., 246. Cf. "Da hat sich, duftig eingeengt / Ein Zicklein aus Gesträuch gehängt / Und *nascht* von jungen Blättern" (Ge., 135).

68 1. Ge., 325.

2. Ge., 264. Cf. "Drei Ritter *prahlen* auf der Wand / Mit rollenden Augen, am Dolch die Hand" (Ge., 320).

3. Ge., 252. Cf. Ge., 350.

4. Ge., 35.

5. Ge., 251.

6. Moser ii, 41.

69 1. Ge., 370.

2. Ge., 381.

3. Korrodi, 54.

70 1. Ge., 377.

2. Ge., 301.

3. Ge., 317; here the initial *h* may have influenced Meyer's choice: "Ein Weiblein *h*inkt mit *H*olz vorbei / Bückt tief sich vor der *H*eil'gen."
4. Ge., 244.

71 1. Ge., 242.
2. Ge., 243.
3. Ge., 265.
4. M., 37–40.
5. "'Eine Predigt Savonarolas,' liess sich der schöne Lelio vernehmen, ein Gähnen verwindend" (V., 23). Similarly: M., 9; A., 27. "'Schach und matt!' krähte der Graf triumphierend." (A. B., 240.)
6. Korrodi, 129–131.
7. Ge., 252.
8. Ge., 253.
9. Ge., 271.
10. Ge., 382.
11. Ge., 309.
12. Hu., 162.
13. Ge., 63.

72 1. R., 403.
2. R., 339.
3. M., 78.
4. M., 91.
5. M., 140.
6. P., 262.
7. G., 308. Cf. also: "wenn eine Person für sich mutterseelen allein *jubelt, fürchtet, verzagt, empfindet, tragirt, imaginirt*." (G., 337.)
8. M., 158.
9. Ge., 304–305.

73 1. Cf. *supra*, page 36, notes 9, 10, 11.
2. *Hengst:* M., 10, 155; *Streithengst:* G., 340, etc.
3. *Stute:* H., 88, etc. *Fuchsstute:* G., 303.
4. *Araber:* H., 38, etc.
5. *Berber:* H., 202; M., 140; V., 173.
6. V., 58. Cf. *das ungrische Fohlen:* G., 336.
7. A. B., 1.
8. *Falber:* A., 9, 20, 22; H., 179, 196, etc.
9. *Brauner:* H., 4, 6, etc.

10. *Fuchs:* Ge., 389; G., 290, 335; J. J., 257, 288, etc.
11. *Rappe:* Ge., 371; A. B., 113; Hu., 27; H., 93, 205; V.,
    173, 185; J. J., 110, 209, 289, 314, etc.
12. *Schimmel:* Ge., 244, 247; "Cäsars *Schimmel* blähn die
    Nüstern," R., 385; J. J., 319; A. B., 199; Hu., 70, 82,
    106, etc.
13. V., 173.
14. H., 82.
15. "seinen goldgeschirrten, tanzenden *Araber*" (H., 38);
    "den arabischen *Schimmel* des Kanzlers" (H., 70); "die
    arabische *Stute* des Kanzlers" (H., 88). Cf. *supra*, page
    36, note 12, and also my article on "Thomas Becket and
    Josef Süss Oppenheimer as Fathers," *The Germanic Re-
    view*, VI, No. 2 (April, 1931), 144–153.
16. "Und da war er! Auf seinem schäumenden *Rappen* in
    der Mitte des leeren Raumes von Allen gemieden"
    (J. J., 289); "Es war Jürg Jenatsch, der seinen unruhigen
    Rappen . . . bändigte"; "auf dem sich bäumenden,
    stampfenden *Rappen*"; "seinen glänzend geschirrten
    Rappen"; "sein feuriger *Rappe*"; "aber angekommen ist
    er, das ist sein *Rappe*" (J. J., 209 *et passim*). Cf. V., 173,
    185, 202.

74 1. M., 68.
    2. M., 71.
    3. V., 18, 54.
    4. V., 32, 38.
    5. M., 62.
    6. M., 57.
    7. M., 56.
    8. M., 74.
    9. M., 77.
   10. M., 127.
   11. M., 90.
   12. M., 9.
   13. M., 55, 56, 115, 120, etc.
   14. M., 164.
   15. R., 278, 334, 364, etc.
   16. Ge., 26.
   17. M., 55.
   18. M., 5.

19. H., 31.
20. J. J., 209.

75 1. R., 291; J. J., 238.
2. R., 274, 293.
3. R., 274, 275.
4. M., 157.
5. A. B., 178.
6. L., 255. For "der Nasige" cf. also L., 243, 249.
7. Cf. *supra*, pages 39–41.

76 1. M., 127.
2. A., 45.
3. A., 108.
4. A. B., 187.
5. Ge., 242.
6. Ge., 243.
7. Ge., 265.
8. Ge., 385.
9. Ge., 144, 298.
10. Ge., 397.
11. Ge., 246.
12. Ge., 12, 122.
13. Ge., 356.
14. Ge., 105, 317.
15. M., 162.
16. So frequently, in fact, as to make tabulation unnecessary.

77 1. M., 104.
2. Ge., 298.
3. Ge., 148.
4. M., 126.
5. A. B., 116.
6. J. J., 111.
7. M., 74.
8. H., 81.
9. M., 141–142.
10. M., 132.
11. M., 115.
12. M., 137. "Überall wird das Zuständliche in Gegenständliches verwandelt, das Innere durch eine geheimnisvolle Symbolik dem Aeussern eingeschlossen. . . . Der Drang zum Gegenständlichen führt zur Betonung des substanti-

vierten Adjektivs . . . und gang besonders des Partizips, d. h. der gegenständlichen Nominalform des zuständlichen Verbums ('sie erfuhren die weggeschleuderte Kutte des Mönchs . . . ohne die vereinigten Hände Dianens und Astorres jedoch')." — Linden, 146; M., 48–49.

78   1. Commenting on Grillparzer's epithets, Stevens (231–232) calls attention to his use of the single adjective. "Medea prophesying an unhappy fate for Kreusa cries:

'Du aber, die hier gleissend steht und heuchelnd
In falscher Reinheit niedersiehst auf mich,
Ich sage dir, du wirst die *weissen* Hände ringen,
Medeens Los beneiden gegen deins.'

It is the adjective *weiss* which gives the passage pictorial power. We may predicate the same of *klein* in the following conversation between Jason and Kreusa:

KREUSA: 'Weisst du, wie ich den Helm aufs Haupt mir setzte?'

JASON: 'Er war zu weit, du hieltst ihn, sanft geduckt, Mit *kleinen* Händen ob den goldnen Locken, Kreusa, es war eine schöne Zeit.'

The same in Naukleros' exhortation to Leander: 'Wein' um die gute, rauf dein *braunes* Haar.' It is the unexpected sensuous detail which brings out the picture."

   2. *Laokoon*, 102.
   3. Ge., 262.
   4. Ge., 158.
   5. Ge., 148.
   6. Ge., 151.
   7. A. B., 17.
   8. H., 138.
   9. V., 122.

79   1. J. J., 40.
   2. J. J., 48.
   3. J. J., 96, 185.
   4. J. J., 93.
   5. J. J., 107.
   6. J. J., 107.
   7. J. J., 107.
   8. J. J., 122.

9. J. J., 185.
10. J. J., 299.
11. J. J., 340.
12. J. J., 107.
13. J. J., 185.

80 1. J. J., 289.
2. J. J., 274. Cf. also J. J., 209.
3. J. J., 124. Cf. also S., 144.
4. Br., II, 63.
5. V., 46.

81 1. *Rheinlande* (October, 1900). On the influence of Ariosto, "probablement l'écrivain qui résume le plus complète-ment l'ensemble d'influences exercées par l'élément latin sur Meyer"; cf. d'Harcourt, 296, footnote 1, also 454–455; Linden, 152; Frey, 177–178.

2. "Als ich ihn bat, mir zu rathen, wie ich den prägnan-testen Ausdruck suchen sollte, wenn der Begriff durch mehrere Worte gedeckt werden konnte, forderte er mich auf die französische Übersetzung der deutschen Rede-weise als sicheren Maasstab zu nehmen." — *Zürcher Taschenbuch*, 1900.

3. "une plasticité, très supérieure à celle de la plupart des romanciers allemands" . . . "cela est sans doute venu à Meyer du commerce des romanciers et des poètes fran-çais" (T. Wyzewa, *Le roman contemporain à l'étranger. Ecrivains étrangers*, 3ᵉ Série [Paris, 1900], 38). On this whole subject cf. Helene V. Lerber, *Der Einfluss der französischen Sprache und Literatur auf C. F. Meyer und seine Dichtung*, Sprache und Dichtung, Heft 29 (Bern [Haupt], 1924).

4. Brw. Meyer-François, 76.

82 1. Cf. Kraeger, *Inhaltsverzeichnis*; Moser, xxiii ff.; Korrodi, 63; d'Harcourt, 306, etc.

2. Brw. Meyer-Rodenberg, 76, 80, 81, 87, 90, 91, 112, 113. Cf. also *ibid.*, 112, 115, 117–119, 129, 245, 247, 256, 257.

83 1. P., 220.
2. Cf. d'Harcourt, 358, footnote 1; also 306.
3. Ge., 201.

84 1. Ge., 34.
2. Frey, 289.
3. Kögel, *Rheinlande* (October, 1900); cf. d'Harcourt, 211, footnote 1.
4. Frey, 287.
5. Cf. among others, d'Harcourt, 307; Everth, 88, "weil er selber augensinnlich angelegt, weil er ein Eidetiker war."
6. Frey, 288.
7. V., 27.
8. Betsy Meyer, 161–165.

85 1. H., 102.
2. M., 68.
3. M., 138.
4. Korrodi, 45

86 1. Betsy Meyer, 187.
2. A. B., 174.
3. V., 186.
4. Ge., 148.
5. V., 30.
6. Ge., 111.
7. M., 2.

87 1. M., 19.
2. Ge., 128.
3. V., 4.
4. R., 304.
5. L., 265.
6. Ge., 379.
7. Ge., 341; A. B., 47.
8. R., 327.
9. V., 57.
10. Ge., 229.
11. Ge., 280. Biblical, cf. Acts v, 9.
12. V., 64.

88 1. R., 319; A. B., 163, etc.
2. R., 355.
3. M., 101.
4. M., 21.
5. Ge., 342; V., 63; R., 375. Cf. also *Zehe*: G., 302.
6. P., 231.
7. L., 182.

8. G., 315.
9. V., 134.
89 1. A. B., 70.
2. M., 11. Cf. also: die wichtige *Miene* (V., 15), die
harmlose *Miene* (V., 46), die kalte *Miene* (V., 91), die
rasende *Miene* (V., 194).
3. Ge., 299.
4. Ge., 313.
5. A. B., 178.
6. V., 76.
7. V., 43. Cf. "mich verlangt in den Bügel." (R., 343.)
8. Ge., 18.
9. V., 90.
10. V., 132.
11. V., 126.
90 1. Ge., 325.
2. M., 9.
3. Ge., 336.
4. M., 154.
5. R., 387.
6. M., 4.
7. M., 8.
8. *Stirn:* Ge., 9, 91, 146, 200, 210, 222, 234, 235, 290, 291,
296, 397, etc., in addition to others listed.
9. A. B., 89.
10. R., 331.
11. Hu., 40.
91 1. G., 277.
2. Ge., 162.
3. Ge., 205.
4. Ge., 335.
5. M., 110.
6. Ge., 292.
7. H., 185.
8. *Lippen:* Ge., 26, 35, 47, 65, 179, 190, 193, 205, 222, 238,
247, 292, 299, 319, 335, 388, etc.; M., 31; V., 123; P., 217;
G., 296, etc.
9. Ge., 225.

10. V., 41. Cf. also for *Mundwinkel*: Ge., 225, 276; V., 16, 41; S., 171; A. B., 48; L., 174, 209, 256; M., 45; G., 293, 306; P., 217, 234, etc.
11. Ge., 346.
12. M., 132.

92
1. V., 136.
2. L., 179.
3. A. B., 51.
4. V., 142.
5. M., 7.
6. Ge., 311.
7. R., 398. Cf. Taylor, 13 ff.; Hellermann, 17 ff., for references to *Augen*.
8. Ge., 229.
9. R., 354.
10. Ge., 371. Cf. also *Ohrlappen*: G., 295.
11. Ge., 391; J. J., 38, *Augenwinkel*.
12. V., 126.
13. Moser, ii, 21.

93
1. Ge., 13.
2. Ge., 226.
3. Ge., 350.
4. Ge., 242.
5. M., 19.
6. *Wimper*: Ge., 13, 205, 226, 317, 339, 350, 379, etc.; E., 41; J. J., 39; A., 5, 12, 116, etc.
7. *Lid*: Ge., 106, 159, 160, 221, 226, 279, 299, 339, 350, 391, etc.; M., 37; R., 397, etc. Cf. for "öffnete die Augen": "Palma, sagte sie zärtlich und dieser warme Klang *hob die Lider* des Kindes, Palma . . ." (R., 397).
8. *Brauen*: Ge., 16, 234, 242, 251, 291, 328, 338, 351, 384, etc., and compare in the stories die buschigen, drohenden, düstern, dunkeln, feinen, finsteren, fröhlichen, gezackten, greisen, hangenden, hochmütigen, hohen, nachdenklichen, pechschwarzen, richtenden, schwarzen, zusammengewachsenen *Brauen*, mentioned: A. B., 6, 21, 173; H., 67, 73, 77, 116, 205, 209; J. J., 14, 33, 85, 101, 120; L., 179, 244, 259; M., 37; P., 254; R., 300, 307, etc. Cf. *infra* (page 111, note 3) the many references to movement of the *Brauen*.

94 1. *Sandra Belloni*, Boxhill ed., 31.
2. *Celt and Saxon*, Boxhill ed., 14.
3. *The Egoist*, Boxhill ed., 10.
4. Richard Aldington, in his poem *Daisy*.
5. Liliencron, *Werke* (Berlin, 1913⁴), II, 40.
6. *Tantris der Narr* (Leipzig, 1911), 30. Cf. also: "O, wie doch ihre rote irländische *Zunge* die Worte wohl zu setzen weiss!" — *Ibid.*, 52.

95 1. *Playboy of the Western World* (Synge, *Works* [Dublin, 1910], II, 104. Cf. also, "winning clean beds and the fill of my belly four times in the day." — *Ibid.*, II, 78.
2. *Deirdre of the Sorrows*, Synge, II, 186.
3. A. B., 56.
4. Ge., 201.
5. V., 71.
6. A. B., 89–90.
7. V., 161.
8. R., 285.
9. R., 338.

96 1. "Ainsi, sans une forme très objective et éminemment artistique, je suis au dedans tout individuel et subjectif. Dans tous les personnages du Pescara, même dans ce vilain Morone, il y a du C. F. M." — Br., I, 138 ff.
2. Ge., 265.
3. P., 234.
4. *Laokoon*, xvii.
5. *Laokoon*, ed. Howard, 111, 118, ll. 12 ff.

97 1. Jonas Cohn, "Die Anschaulichkeit der dichterischen Sprache," *Ztft. f. Ä.*, II, 182–201.
M. Dessoir, "Anschauung und Beschreibung," *Archiv f. systematische Phil.*, X, 20 ff.
K. Groos, "Das Anschauliche Vorstellen beim poetischen Gleichnis," *Ztft. f. Ä.*, IX, 186–207.
T. A. Meyer, *Das Stilgesetz der Poesie* (Leipzig, 1901), *passim*.
R. Müller-Freienfels, *Psychologie der Kunst* (Leipzig, 1912), *passim*; esp., I, 67 ff., II, 89 ff.
H. Roetteken, "Zur Lehre von den Darstellungsmitteln in der Poesie," *Ztft. f. v. Lit.*, N. F. 4, 17 ff. (1891).

J. Volkelt, *System der Ästhetik* (München, 1905), I, Bd. 3.
Abschitt, 5. Kap.: Die Anschaulichkeit in der Dichtung,
412–428.
J. E. Downey, *The Imaginal Reaction to Poetry*, Univ.
of Wyoming, Psy. Bulletin, No. 2 (1912).

2. Karl Groos ("Das Anschauliche Vorstellen beim poetischen Gleichniss," *Ztft. f. Ä.*, IX [1914], 207) closes his discussion with the comment: "Diese Beispiele zeigen wohl
deutlich, dass man das Problem des 'anschaulichen' Vors-
tellens nicht auf das visuelle Gebiet beschränken darf. Und
sie zeigen ebenso deutlich, was ich schon im Anfang dieses
Aufsatzes betonte; auch im Reiche des Schönen kann
man nach recht verschiedener Façon selig werden."

3. F. Th. Vischer believed: "Wer dem inneren Auge nichts
gibt, wer ihm nicht zeichnen kann, ist kein Dichter."
This is, so far as I am aware, the orthodox attitude
toward the subject in the customary chapter on description in the American textbooks on rhetoric. Young, *Fresh-
man English* (1914), 430: "A literary description aims to
create in the mind of another person an image of the
thing seen by the describer, an image which must not
only be accurate, but which must also convey some distinctive aesthetic impression." — Not so the advanced
aesthetician, who asks: "Wer hätte die Zeit, wenn die
Worte an ihm vorübergleiten, die gedehnte Handlung,
die als einheitliche Tatsache in ihnen ausgesprochen ist,
gewisserwassen aufzublättern und ihre einzelnen Teile
in der gebührenden Reihenfolge zu beschauen?" (T. A.
Meyer, 56.) His question is echoed by Volkelt (415):
"Wie wäre es denn auch, besonders bei raschem Lesen
oder beim Hören der von Schauspieler oft rasend schnell
gesprochenen Worte möglich all die — noch dazu oft
recht verwickelten — Phantasieanschauungen, die den
einzelnen Worten entsprechen, der Reihe nach zu
erzeugen?"

Schopenhauer (*Die Welt als Wille und Vorstellung*,
Sect. 9) seems to anticipate the moderns: "es ist nicht
nötig, ja nicht einmal erwünscht, das sich überall
'Phantasmen' einmengen — welch ein 'Tumult' wäre
sonst in unserem Kopfe."

Nor is the conjuring up of appropriate images at all necessary. Cf. Groos (186): "sehr starke und vollkommene poetische Eindrücke sind auch ohne die Erregung innerer Bilder möglich"; Cohn (201): "Die Wörter der Sprache erzeugen höchst selten und nur bei wenigen Menschen vollständig bestimmte Bilder. . . . Die poetische Sprache . . . erzeugt (aber) . . . in der Tat eine Anschauung wenn wir dies Wort nur richtig verstehen. Anschauung im ästhetischen Sinne ist ein in sich ruhendes volles Erleben." — Even a conservative aesthetician, like Johannes Volkelt, who has written three large volumes under the title *System der Ästhetik*, considers most essential, not the mental image, but the feeling of sureness of our ability to construct such an image — to paraphrase what he expresses by means of a formidable, not to say forbidding, nine-syllable word. I quote Volkelt (417, Sect. 7): "Wir empfinden als Phantasieanschaulichkeit nicht bloss das ausdrückliche Phantasiesehen und Phantasiehören, sondern auch die betonte Gewissheit der Phantasieanschauungsmöglichkeit."

4. Goethe, *Faust*, II, 8691–8692.
5. Gubelman, 70, footnote 17.
6. *PMLA* (1911) 598.
7. *Laokoon*, ed. Howard, 130.
8. Galton, *Inquiries into Human Faculty*, 83–114.

98 1. Müller-Freienfels, 91. Cf. also Volkelt, 421: "Die Bedeutung der Bewegungsempfindung für die Anschaulichkeit in der Dichtung."
2. *Troilus and Cressida*, III, 3, Ulysses speaking.
3. *Laokoon*, ed. Howard, 134.
4. Müller-Freienfels, 91. Cf. also Volkelt, 421, etc.
5. Notable examples of description in the manner which Lessing approves in Homer, are to be found in Kleist, *Der Zerbrochene Krug*, vii Auftritt, Frau Marthe spricht; Goethe, *Hermann und Dorothea*, Canto iv, ll. 1 ff.; Schiller, *Spaziergang*, etc.
6. *Laokoon*, xiv.
7. *Laokoon*, xv.

99 1. *Laokoon*, ed. Howard, 99.
2. H., 43.

3. *Laokoon*, ed. Howard, 96.

4. H., 92.

100 1. H., 215. Meyer's representations of his characters even when in action sometimes seem to aim at reminiscences of plastic art. So Hans der Armbruster portrays Thomas Becket (H., 44): "Jetzt erhob sich aus einer tiefen Nische" (where statues most often stand) "ein vornehmer, bleicher Mann" (statues are usually colorless and aristocratic in bearing) "in köstlichen Gewanden" (statues are commonly clad in drapery of no particular historical style whose folds may suggest motion) "und trat, diese schön und langsam bewegend, zu mir, als trüge er Verlangen" (just so a statue looks and by suggestion moves as though it had a conscious purpose) "Ihr stellt des Leids Gebärde dar,/Ihr meine Kinder, ohne Leid!" (Ge., 335.)

2. R., 290.

3. R., 403.

4. R., 274; cf. Everth, 23.

5. Ge., 250.

6. V., 167.

7. R., 370. Cf. a similar passage in Meredith, *The Tragic Comedians*, ed. Scribner, 51: "His eyes *dilated, steadied, speculated, weighed* her"; or Dehmel, *Tragische Erscheinung*: "ein grosser Tropfen Blut *quoll, hing* und *fiel.*"

8. M., 90.

101 1. M., 107–108.

2. Ge., 159. Cf. also Ge., 63, 155, 159, 188, 250, 380, etc.; R., 290, 403; P., 26; G., 337; M., 140, etc.

3. Scherer, *Poetik*, 263.

4. Cf. Stevens, 230, "on the value of the verb as a descriptive agent."

102 1. P., 225.

2. M., 143.

3. Cf. my article on "Conrad Ferdinand Meyer in Recent Translation," *MLJ*, XV, No. 8 (May, 1931), 581–590.

103 1. H., 57, 58.

2. V., 15.

3. R., 331. A similar emphasis on action is characteristic of the style of George Meredith, which I hope before long to analyze elsewhere.

4. F. Hellermann, *Mienenspiel und Gebärdensprache in C. F. Meyers Novellen*, Diss. Giessen (Hamburg, 1912), 77 pp., a work which is restricted in range by the subtitle, "Die Ausdrucksbewegungen mit besonderer Berücksichtigung des Auges"; in scope, by the rather arbitrary selection of certain *Novellen* (cf. 16). There is much better treatment of the same material, "Meyers Gebärdenkunst und Gebärdensprache" in Korrodi (32 ff.), and much better selection and arrangement of material in the few pages in d'Harcourt on "le geste parenthèse" (479 ff.). Cf. also Wera Kostowa, *Die Bewegungen und Haltungen des menschlichen Körpers in C. F. Meyers Erzählungen*, Diss. Tübingen (Leipzig, 1915), and Joh. Bathe, *Die Bewegung und Haltung des menschlichen Körpers in H. v. Kleists Erzählungen*, Diss. Tübingen (1917).

5. Kögel, *Rheinlande*, October, 1900. Cf. Br., II, 222; also d'Harcourt, 389, footnote 3, 373, footnote 1, 522–523; Baumgarten, 163; Hans Corrodi, 95; Korrodi, 154; Linden, 152–153.

6. d'Harcourt, 298–299, 477 ff. Cf. Hans Käslin, "C. F. Meyer und Prosper Mérimée" (*Wissen und Leben* [November 15, 1918], 133–143).

7. d'Harcourt, 480.

104 1. Not of Don Giulio, as Korrodi (29) incorrectly states.

2. A. B., 106.

3. V., 118.

4. M., 94.

5. A., 86.

6. J. J., 63.

7. Hu., 150.

8. V., 33.

9. V., 173.

10. V., 77.

11. V., 194.

12. P., 225.

13. H., 27.

14. A. B., 110.

105 1. d'Harcourt, 478: "Statistique instructive à faire du nombre de fois que Meyer a employé le mot, *Geberde*."

2. Hellermann has examined only seven of Meyer's *Novellen* (cf. 16). Instead of exercising a wise principle of selection, he tries to be exhaustive and forces the large mass of his material into an outline, the *fundamentum divisionis* of which is difficult to fathom, and which succeeds only in mystifying the reader and in obscuring the most interesting part of his investigation. "Eine Zahlenmässige Vergleichung ergibt, dass in den sieben Novellen die Ausdrucksbewegung allein 156 mal steht, in Verbindung mit der Rede 173 mal." —Hellermann, 44.

3. In the poems mention is made of "Eine allumarmende, atmende, freche, gelassene, lässige, überredende, zürnende Geberde." Cf. for *Geberde* in the poems: Ge., 110, 149, 197, 226, 236, 244, 256, 259, 335; E., 69, 90; Hu., 73, etc.

4. In the prose mention is made of "Eine abwehrende, ängstliche, ausdrucksvolle, bittende, demonstrierende, demüthige, dictatorische, edle, ehrfürchtige, empörende, entrüstete, entzückte, ermuthigende, erzürnte, feindselige, flehende, flüchtige, freche, furchtsame, gebieterische, gewaltige, griffelhaltende, halbgierige, halbherablassende, haschende, heftige, hochfahrende, inbrünstige, krampfhafte, krönende, kurzsichtige, leidenschaftliche, liebende, männliche, mönchische, nachahmende, possenhafte, rasende, ruhige, schmeichelnde, starke, steife, stolze, tragische, trotzige, ungeduldige, ungezügelte, unterthänige, unwiderstehliche, verzweifelte, verurtheilende, weite, wichtige, widerwillige, zerstreute Geberde." Cf. for *Geberde* in the prose: A., 52, 53, 60, 65, 97, 112; A. B., 20, 66, 77, 181, 202; G., 277, 284, 293, 303, 320, 323, 330, 332, 353; H., 13, 52, 77, 107, 146, 174, 179, 197, 215, 231; J. J., 27, 33, 46, 62, 70, 118, 160, 305, 338; L., 210, 241, 272; M., 12, 13, 18, 20, 32, 43, 51, 58, 85, 97, 98, 129, 140, 146, 148, 158; R., 285, 311, 317, 326, 331, 337, 351, 374; S., 139, 159, 178, 192, 212; V., 2, 15, 27, 36, 44, 45, 56, 62, 68, 76, 81, 97, 112, 146, 168, 197, 198, etc. Cf. also compounds such as: Dankgeberde, Fluchgeberde, Grussgeberde, Machtgeberde, Mordgeberde, Siegesgeberde, etc.; and the use of the verb, sich *geberden*: H., 167, 169, 193; L., 249; M., 145; V., 91, 203, etc.

5. A., 100. Cf. Ge., 299.

6. M., 67, 68; A. B., 86, 144.
7. H., 49–50 (three times).
8. A. B., 9, 10, 11, 44, 65.
9. J. J., 304.
10. G., 324.
11. M., 104.
12. Stevens, *Grillparzer*, 240.

106 1. R., 284.
2. H., 232.
3. L., 220.
4. P., 256, 257.
5. S., 150.
6. M., 144.

107 1. Grillparzer, *Werke*[5], ed. Sauer, xi, 20.
2. V., 210.
3. P., 230.

108 1. V., 37.
2. J. J., 308.
3. A., 29.
4. M., 108.   Cf. a very similar passage, R., 277.
5. A. B., 36.
6. A. B., 78.

109 1. V., 202.
2. V., 116.
3. M., 57.
4. A. B., 92.   Cf. also: "Der Bravo zeigte lächelnd die weissen Zähne und lüftete den Dolch, der ihm am Gurt hing, ein wenig in der Scheide" (A. B., 54).
5. J. J., 33–34.
6. H., 231.

110 1. Ge., 299.
2. H., 60.
3. H., 201.
4. M., 85.
5. V., 173.   Korrodi, 33.
6. Hu., xviii; d'Harcourt, 480: "Otto von Gemmingen donne à entendre à Hutten malade, par un geste symbolique tracé par le doigt autour du cou, qu'une existence dont les heures sont ainsi comptées doit être héroique-

ment employée. La pièce portera le titre significatif de 'Die Geberde.'"

7. M., 12; cf. Everth, 78.
8. V., 92.

III　1. A. B., 67.
2. d'Harcourt, 479.
3. "Zog die Brauen in die Höhe" (cf. R., 276, 292; A., 19; J. J., 310, etc.); "Zog die Brauen zusammen" (cf. A. B., 27, 181, 208; L., 180, 230; M., 100; S., 154; A., 75; J. J., 110, 205, 208, 213, etc.); cf. also for *Brauen*: V., 27, 147; M., 69; H., 75, 100; A. B., 67; E., 25, 89, etc.
4. S., 178.
5. On Meyer and Lavater cf. d'Harcourt, 146, 147.
6. "Wie immer bei diesem Dichter, der alles Innere ins Äussere übersetzen muss, charakterisiert sie schon die äussere Erscheinung: beide von hohem Wuchse, ist Diane herbe, streng, verschlossen gegen Ihresgleichen . . . Germano ist rauh, herausfahrend, ungeschickt." — Linden, 88; Kalischer, 155 ff.

II2　1. V., 57–58.
2. V., 65–66.
3. H., 224.
4. Kalischer, 157.
5. M., 40.
6. Korrodi, 31 ff.; Kalischer, 159 ff.; I have without difficulty doubled the examples there given.
7. V., 135.
8. A., 52.

II3　1. V., 122.
2. M., 23.
3. P., 260.
4. L., 205.
5. L., 230.

II4　1. Lessing, *Laokoon,* ed. Howard, 133.
2. J. Cohn, *Ztft. f. Ä.*, II, 196.
3. Frey, 288. H. G. Wells in *Mr. Britling Sees It Through* would describe a character not alone through the effect he makes on his fellow actors but on nature itself. Of Colonel Rendezvous, who is "presented as a monster of energy and self-discipline; as the determined foe of every

form of looseness, slackness, and easy-goingness," the
example of efficiency, Kitchenerism, in fine, he says (76):
"When he walks down the park all the plants dress in-
stinctively. . . . And there's a tree near their gate; it used
to be a willow. You can ask any old man in the village.
But ever since Rendezvous took the place it's been trying
to present arms. With the most extraordinary results.
I was passing the other day with old Windershin. 'You
see that there old poplar,' he said; 'It's a willow' said I.
'No,' he said, 'it did use to be a willow before Colonel
Rendezvous he came. But now it's a poplar.' . . . And
by Jove, it *is* a poplar!"

4. "In the description, Machaut follows the enumerative
method so dear to the Middle Ages, as if he were, in Hamlet's phrase, 'dividing' the lady 'inventorially.'"—G. L.
Kittredge, *Chaucer*, 64.

5. I. Babbitt, *The New Laokoön*, Boston & New York
(1910); L., 30.

6. Lessing, *Laokoon*, ed. Howard, 113.

7. *Ibid.*, 108.

115 1. *Laokoon*, ed. Howard, 262. Erstes Wäldchen, XIII.

2. Lessing, *Laokoon*, ed. Howard, 102.

3. M., 5.

4. L., 173. Cf. also L., 217.

5. J. J., 274.

116 1. *Ztft. f. Ä.*, II, 197 and footnote.

2. H., 43.

3. H., 74.

4. A. B., 147.

5. The difference between describing laboriously in the
manner condemned by Lessing and describing concisely,
stressing personal reaction, the method of Meyer, is admirably illustrated in two descriptions of the interior of
Durham Cathedral, one by Hawthorne, the other by Dr.
Johnson. While Hawthorne gives a laborious, lengthy
enumeration of detail — a mere inventory of things
seen, taking pains to comment even on such minutiae as
the ornamentations of the pillars, "some are wrought
with chevrons like those on the sleeve of a police inspec-
tor"—and presents a mass of material, which the gentle

reader, sick through surfeit of too much and probably only a poor visualizer at best, cannot possibly assimilate, much less reconstruct into a picture, Dr. Johnson sums up the whole situation in a single sentence: "The Cathedral has a massiness and solidity such as I have seen in no other place; it rather awes than pleases, as it strikes with a kind of gigantic dignity, and aspires to no other praise than that of rocky solidity and indeterminate duration." The best parts of Hawthorne's detailed description are those which express a similar subjective reaction. "The effect is to give the edifice an air of heavy grandeur . . . it weighs upon the soul, instead of helping it to aspire." These two descriptions, to which Mr. F. W. C. Hersey kindly called my attention, may be found in Hawthorne, *English Note-Books* (July 11, 1837), and Dr. Johnson, *Letters*, ed. B. Hill, I, 226 (Aug. 12, 1773).

117 1. V., 28.

2. V., 174.

3. A. B., 177.

4. A. B., 226.

5. H., 185–186.

118 1. H., 195. Similarly in *Die Hochzeit des Mönchs*: "Dante lauschte. Der Wind pfiff um die Ecken der Burg und stiess einen schlecht verwahrten Laden auf. Monte Baldo hatte seine ersten Schauer gesendet. Man sah die Flocken stäuben und wirbeln, von der Flamme des Herdes beleuchtet. Der Dichter betrachtete den Schneesturm und seine Tage, welche er sich entschlüpfen fühlte, erschienen ihm unter der Gestalt dieser bleichen Jagd und Flucht durch eine unstete Röthe. Er bebte vor Frost. Und seine feinfühligen Zuhörer empfanden mit ihm, dass ihn kein eigenes Heim, sondern nur wandelbare Gunst wechselnder Gönner bedache und vor dem Winter beschirme, welcher Landstrasse und Feldweg mit Schnee bedeckte. Alle wurden es inne und Cangrande, der von grosser Gesinnung war, zuerst: Hier sitzt ein Heimatloser!" (M., 91–92.) Cf. on this whole subject, Emil Brack, *Die Landschaft in C. F. Meyers Novellen und Gedichten*, Diss. Bern (Leipzig, 1925).

2. Korrodi, 154–155.

3. Wüst, 146–147: "Man kann wohl von einer gewissen *Möbellust* sprechen." Korrodi (19 ff.), writing ten excellent pages on the significance of works of art in Meyer's stories, makes the assertion, "Er [Meyer] benutzt ein Bild nie anders, denn als Mittel zum Zweck." So true this assertion is that Korrodi need not have stated, "Gewiss wird hier und da ein Kunstwerk in einem Gemache aufgestellt, ohne dass es in bedeutsame Beziehung mit dessen Bewohnern gebracht wird" (20). Certainly he falls into error in his only illustration of this statement: "Jene Venus aus der Tizianschule beim Provveditore erfüllt lediglich den Zweck einer Zimmergarnitur." He means the statue mentioned in *Jürg Jenatsch*, II, 6 (J. J., 153). Had he read on a paragraph further, he would have found the statue "in bedeutsame Beziehung gebracht" with the characters, serving here the purpose of indirect characterization of Waser; for in the very second sentence following mention of the statue, we read: "[Waser] hatte sogar versäumt seinen Stuhl so zu setzen, dass er dem verlockenden Götterbilde den Rücken zuwandte, was er sonst nie zu thun vergass."

119 1. H., 184–185.

2. H., 151–152. In the same story (H., 177) Medusa is dragged in, one may say, by the very snakes of her head, in order to have a reference to a bit of sculpture discovered on the market-place of Arles.

3. A. B., 7.

120 1. A. B., 184.

2. V., 152. In the same story he characterizes his persons by their attitude toward food at table. Guicciardin, "gelb und gallig," "wies eine süsse Schüssel zurück und bereitete sich mit mehr Essig als Oel einen Gurkensalat," ... "während der schöne Lälius ein Zuckerbrot zerbröckelte." (V., 18–19, 21–22.)

3. Frey, 287–288.

121 1. Baumgarten, 142: "Dies instinktive und unbewusste Kompensationsstreben."

123 1. "Jürg Jenatsch. Niemals wieder hat Meyer einen Vertreter des ästhetisch-konkreten Prinzips in solcher Rein- und Bestimmtheit vor Augen gestellt." — Linden, 77.

"Thomas Becket. Er ist der bedeutendste und durchgebildetste Vertreter des abstrakten Prinzips, den Meyer geschaffen hat." — Linden, 79.

"Wie Jürg Jenatsch die grossartigste Verkörperung des ästhetisch-konkreten, so ist der Heilige in seiner unheimlichen Zweideutigkeit der gewaltigste Vertreter des ethisch-abstrakten Prinzips, den Meyer geschaffen hat." — Linden, 87.

2. Br., II, 66. Cf. Maync, 74; Baumgarten (53) becomes epigrammatic: "In Meyers Bild ist die Renaissance von der Reformation angekränkelt und beseelt."

3. Jürg Jenatsch – Herzog Rohan, Heinrich II – Thomas Becket, Lucrezia Borgia – Angela Borgia. — Linden, 5, 78.

4. "Die Analyse der grossen Novellen wie die Betrachtung der grossen Entwürfe lässt überall das *Grunderlebnis* des Dichters erkennen: der Gegensatz des ästhetisch-konkreten und ethisch-abstrakten Geistes, der Meyers Entwicklung beherrscht, hat in seinen Dichtungen *Gestalt* gewonnen." — Linden, 119.

5. "Eine innere Leidenschaft, im Leben tief verborgen und unterdrückt, gelangt im Kunstwerk zum erlösenden Ausdruck"; "das ist der Dichter in seiner Aussenseite, die die drängende Leidenschaft des Innern verbirgt und verhüllt." — Linden, 4–5.

"Der wahre Meyer ist derjenige der Tat, der Leidenschaft, der Sinnlichkeit, der Persönlichkeit." — Linden, 231.

124   1. "Und so heisst das grosse Gesetz seines Lebens: *Synthese.*" — Linden, 7, also 154.

2. Linden, 51. "Man ist . . . so weit gegangen, den Menschen Meyer, mit seiner Sehnsucht zu verwechseln, und es ist vor allem der Irrtum von Lindens tüchtigem Buch, zu behaupten, in dem äusserlich scheuen, verschlossenen, tatlosen und unbewegten Menschen habe innen eine verborgene Leidenschaft geglüht." — Faesi, 144.

3. Everth, 257.

4. Faesi, 132.

125   1. Everth, 118.

2. Br., I, 182.

3. Frey, 307, 422.

126 1. Brw. Meyer-Rodenberg, 66, letter of April 21, 1880. Cf. Faesi, 139; Maync, 87; Unger, *Aufsätze zur Literatur- und Geistesgeschichte* (Berlin, 1929), 207.

2. Thomas Mann, *Fiorenza*, Nov. II, 219. Cf. Faesi, 144.

3. Unger, *Aufsätze*, 207.

4. Maync, 87; Faesi, 139.

5. Faesi, 139.

6. E., 93; Faesi, 131. "So suchte auch Meyer Schutz vor dem eigenen Ich, das, sich selbst überlassen, ihn zu sprengen drohte. Wie er in der Objektivität der visuellen Anschauung Ruhe und Konzentration fand, so in der Geschichte, fern von seinem Alltag" (Everth, 223); and also "auf der einen Seite der Drang und die Begabung zur anschaulichen Vergegenwärtigung, zur sinnlichen Verkörperung und insofern Wirklichkeitsnähe; und daneben liegen Bedürfnisse der Fernung, der Zurückhaltung und dadurch vertiefter Innerlichkeit, und beides widerstrebt sich nicht." (Everth, 61–62.)

127 1. Brw. Meyer-François, 3. Cf. d'Harcourt, 231, footnote 2.

2. Everth, 116.

3. d'Harcourt, 231. Before him, to be sure, I. Sadger had pointed out, "Weil Konrad Meyer sich klein und schwach und unfähig fühlte, erbärmlich behandelt von seiner Umgebung, drum sucht er sein Heil in der Renaissance mit ihren Kolossalgestalten."—*Konrad Ferdinand Meyer. Eine pathographisch-psychologische Studie. Grenzfragen des Nerven und Seelenlebens*, LIX (Wiesbaden, 1908).

4. Brw. Meyer-François, 159. Cf. d'Harcourt, 232, footnote 1.

5. d'Harcourt, 132, 232, 335.

6. d'Harcourt, 121 ff., 321; Faesi, 33.

7. d'Harcourt (124), apparently in error, writes Angela for Lucrezia Borgia.

128 1. In writing "Denn [König Heinrich] besitzt die Eigenschaft aller ästhetisch-konkreten Menschen, vergangene Dinge hinter sich werfen zu können, wie es Lucrezia Borgia, Stemma, Astorre und Jenatsch tun," Linden (78) did not realize that Meyer may here have expressed an unconscious desire to do the same.

2. M., 104–105. Cf. d'Harcourt, 231, footnote 2; Maync, 69.

3. d'Harcourt, 197, footnote 2.
4. Brw. Meyer-François, 32. Cf. also "Ich gehe mit Kaiser u. Reich durch Dick u. Dünn." — Brw. Meyer-Rodenberg, 242.
5. Brw. Meyer-François, 105. Inaccurately cited in exaggerated form by Baumgarten, 69.
6. Br., I, 128.
7. "[Nietzsche] pries, was ihm fehlte, wie zum Beispiele auch C. F. Meyer die Gewaltmenschen verherrlichte und das Gegentheil davon war." (Möbius, *Nietzsche*, 37.) This principle of over-compensation Everth (50) applies even to vocabulary: "Hinter Superlativen steht nicht selten eine schwache Position. . . . So verrät der Mann der grossen Worte oft gerade sein kleines Kaliber." Cf. Maync, 73.

129 1. "Il est impossible de comprendre Meyer sans voir en lui le névrosé qu'il était héréditairement et qu'il resta toute sa vie, avec deux crises particulièrement graves qui le mèneront à l'asile. Ces deux crises, se produisant à vingt-sept et à soixante-sept ans, se trouvent pour ainsi dire encadrer son existence." — d'Harcourt, 24–25.
2. *Lettres de C. F. Meyer et de son entourage* (Paris, 1913).
3. d'Harcourt, *Crise*, Introduction, i.
4. Frey, 304; d'Harcourt, 24; Everth, 275; Lusser, 16. "Die neurasthenische Angst und der Selbsterhaltungstrieb des Schwachen zwangen Meyer Distanz zu halten vom Leben." — Baumgarten, 152.
5. "Elizabeth Meyer, pour la première fois, nomme le mal et dénonce chez son fils la disposition hyponcondriaque; elle trace une silhouette fort exacte et presque classique de la neurasthénie: mélancolie, préoccupations de santé, irrégularité et irrésolution d'existence, sauvagerie misanthropique, intensité déréglée de la vie imaginative." — d'Harcourt, 37.
6. "'Mein erstes, mein begabtes Kind ist für solche Zukunftshoffnungen einer Mutter verloren! Er begräbt sich selbst. Er ist für dieses Leben nicht mehr da. . . .' Und mein armer Bruder hörte das." — Betsy Meyer, 102.
7. d'Harcourt, 35; Maync, 217.
8. Faesi, 20.

130 1. "Was mich niederwarf und aufrieb, war die Missachtung, das Für krank gelten . . . jene Hinweisung auf meine . . . unverschuldete Berufslosigkeit." (Letter to Betsy) — Frey, 87.

2. In a letter of June 1, 1853, she scolds him for buying expensive shoes, sends him a razor but cautions him not to wipe it on his handkerchiefs in which he has cut holes but only on the little cloths she encloses, and warns him to be careful with his pocket money (Frey, 68–70; d'Harcourt, *Crise*, 100). D'Harcourt (98) concludes: "Conrad (il nous faut avoir le courage de le répéter après M. Sadger) voyait disparaître en même temps que la plus tendre des mères un des principaux obstacles à son développement"; Frey (70) remarks: "Der Siebenundzwanzigjährige wird fortwährend ermahnt, zurechtgewiesen, geschulmeistert bedauert und drangsaliert mit Kleinigkeiten, die man einem an den Nerven Angegriffenen ersparen muss."

3. In a letter to his confidante Cécile Borrel of November 24, 1855, Meyer makes the following analysis of his misfortunes: "Entouré de jeunes hommes, jadis mes camarades, qui tous sont arrivés ou arrivent à quelque chose, cherchant à me rattacher partout et n'y réussissant que rarement, regardé de haut en bas par des hommes qui peutêtre, ne me valent pas, soupçonné par qui ne m'aime pas de n'être point encore entièrement guéri, contraint de m'humilier incessament, ce qui ne m'est pas naturel du tout, je suis souvent très malheureux." — d'Harcourt, *Crise*, 248.

4. Frey, 304.

5. Frey, 305; d'Harcourt, 264; Faesi, 28–29.

6. "Zumal von seiner verlorenen Jugend sprach er ungern." — Everth, 275.

7. Br., I, 138.

8. Brw. Meyer-François, 48.

9. "Ein Lieblingswort C. F. Meyers ist 'die Maske'." — Korrodi, 108. Cf. Maync, 89.

131 1. d'Harcourt, 240, footnote 1. Cf. Frey, 51: "sonst floh er Gesellschaft, namentlich weibliche"; also Br., II, 165.

2. Everth, 114.

3. Br., I, 139. I expect to return to this subject in a forth-
coming article to be entitled "Conrad Ferdinand Meyer
Unmasks Himself."

132 1. G., 275. Later (G., 291) called "Casse-Cou."

2. Maync, 341, and Everth, 311: "Er hat eine Reihe un-
vergesslicher Männergestalten geschaffen, doch nur eine
ebenbürtige Frau: Lucrezia Borgia." Cf. Fritz Dom-
merich, *Die Frauengestalten in den Novellen C. F. Meyers*
(Rostock, 1928).

3. d'Harcourt, 420–422.

133 1. V., 130. Cf. Linden, 6, and on the general subject of
fatalism in Meyer, Ernst Feise, *Fatalismus als Grundzug
von C. F. Meyers Werken*, Euphorion, Bd. 17 (1910),
111–143.

2. Faesi, 134.

134 1. Betsy Meyer, 14: "So war eines seiner Lieblingsbücher
die Selbstbiographie des Benvenuto Cellini, die er immer
wieder las und unvergleichlich nannte." Cf. d'Harcourt,
215, footnote 1, and O. Blaser, "C. F. Meyer und Benvenuto Cellini," *Neues Jahresblatt d. lit. Gesellschaft Bern*
(1917), 85.

2. A. B., 106.

3. Linden, 152.

135 1. Everth, 281.

2. R., 374. Cf. also Otto Rank, *Das Inzest Motiv in Dichtung and Sage* (Leipzig und Wien, 1912), 523 ff.

136 1. Everth, 114, 303.

2. Baumgarten, 121.

3. Schiller, *Sämtliche Werke*, Säkularausgabe, III, 116.

4. Frey, 53, 54, 198–199, 228, 250, 252, etc., and d'Harcourt,
Crise, 203, postscript to a letter of July 22, 1853, "Ich
grüsse den l. Herrn Mallet und dem Pizz einen kleinen
Gruss auf seinen unwiderstehlichen Hintern."

5. Betsy Meyer, 182.

137 1. *Ibid.*, 6. She is referring, to be sure, to his relations
with Gottfried Kinkel and Caroline Bauer, both robust,
imposing, and dominating personalities. *Ibid.*, 8: "So
bewegten sich schwächer oder spröder organisierte
Naturen, wenn sie der Zufall neben diese alten Voll-
blutsmenschen versetzte, ganz unwillkürlich etwas rück-

wärts, teils wohl um von ihrer Art nicht psychisch
Gewalt zu erleiden, teils auch im Gefühle, sie müssten,
damit man ihnen gerecht würde, in einem weiteren
Rahmen stehen und wie Freskobilder aus einer gewissen
Ferne betrachtet werden können." Baumgarten (152)
somewhat cavalierly applies this generalization to Meyer,
probably not without justification in fact, however. Cf.
Frey (51): "Er hatte es ungern, wenn man ihm nahe auf
den Leib rückte, und bot zum Gruss immer nur zwei
Finger der rechten Hand." Cf. also (G., 285): "Ich bin
ein Freund der Reserve und ein Feind naher Berührung."

2. Betsy Meyer, 9.

138 1. A. B., 57–58.

2. Cf. the statements of typical characters in Grillparzer's
dramas; e. g., Ottokar in *König Ottokars Glück und Ende*,
ll. 2833–2835, 2868–2869; Rustan in *Der Traum ein
Leben*, ll. 2653–2659; Medea in *Das goldene Vlies*, ll. 2372–
2373: "Was ist der Erde Glück? — Ein Schatten! / Was
ist der Erde Ruhm? — Ein Traum!"

3. A. B., 67. Cf. Frey, 308; Maync, 73–74; Baumgarten, 87.

139 1. Betsy Meyer, 28.

2. Frey, 283; Faesi, 131.

3. J. J., 287.

4. Ge., 27–33. Cf. Maync, 70.

5. Cf. Hebbel, *Sämmtliche Werke*, Säkularausgabe, XI, 9:
"Ich will nur den weitverbreiteten Wahn, als ob der
Dichter etwas Anderes geben könne, als sich selbst, als
seinen eigenen Lebensprocess, bestreiten."

6. Linden (154) finds Meyer's art to be "die Synthese einer
Antithese," with which judgment I am unable to agree
for reasons set forth in the text above.

140 1. Ge., 326–327.

141 1. Brw. Meyer-Rodenberg, 189. Cf. Korrodi, 115; Everth, 44.

2. Everth, 45.

3. Brw. Meyer-Rodenberg, 223. Cf. Maync, 277.

4. "und ich hasse die Breite, die sogenannte Fülle." — Br.,
I, 447.

5. Brw. Meyer-Rodenberg, 226–227: "Gerade an einer
gewissen Breite u. Fülle liegt es mir dieses Mal." Cf.
Ibid., 238, 242.

142 1. V., 44.

2. R. L. Stevenson, *Technical Elements of Style*, Biog. ed. (N. Y., 1905), 259.

3. Ge., 3.

143 1. Carl Busse, "Der Maskenträger," *Neue Freie Presse* (March 27, 1917).

2. Arthur Eloesser, "C. F. Meyers literarische Beisetzung," *Lit. Echo*, XX, No. 2 (October 15, 1917), 80–83.

3. F. F. Baumgarten, *Das Werk Conrad Ferdinand Meyers, Renaissance-Empfinden und Stilkunst* (München [Georg Müller], 1920²). Cf. *supra*, page 8, footnote 1.

4. Baumgarten, 77, 81, 84, 85, 86.

5. *Ibid.*, 24, 45–46, 88, 89, 127, 175.

144 1. *Ibid.*, 199, 200.

2. *Ibid.*, 13, 48, 153, 187. Rodenberg earlier wrote to Meyer, "Ich möchte Sie keinen Romantiker nennen, sondern ein Renaissancedichter." — Brw. Meyer-Rodenberg, 135.

3. The title of Rudolf Unger's article on Meyer, *Die Literatur*, XXVI, No. 6 (March, 1924), 321–324, No. II of the series *Moderne Strömungen in der deutschen Literaturwissenschaft*.

145 1. Cf. my summary of this controversy, *JEGP*, XXVII, No. 4 (October, 1928), 486–495, from which I have made selections for the text above.

2. "In rein aesthetischer Hinsicht wird wohl von dem strengen Urteil Baumgartens, trotz Everths Widerspruch, schwerlich allzuviel abzudingen sein." — Rudolf Unger, *C. F. Meyer. Eine Charakteristik zu seinem Säculartage* in Festschrift für Max Koch (Breslau [Preuss u. Jünger], 1926), 123.

3. "Die Lyrik C. F. Meyers," *Ztft. f. Aesthetik*, Bd. 7 (1912), pp. 372–396.

4. Brw. Keller-Storm, ed. Köster², 132.

5. *Ibid.*, 162 (December 22, 1882).

6. *Hausbuch aus deutschen Dichtern seit Claudius*, Eine kritische Anthologie (Hamburg, 1870).

146 1. Brw. Keller-Storm, ed. Köster², 172 (March 13, 1883).

2. Frey, 308–309, 328.

3. Faesi, 38. Cf. Meyer's own sentiments (Ge., 335), "So sieht der freigewordne Geist / Des Lebens überwundne Qual."

4. Baumgarten, 199–200.

5. Br., II, 31.

147   1. Frey, 167–168.

2. d'Harcourt (305–306): "Le résultat de cette élaboration méticuleuse et savante, le fruit de cette inlassable conscience d'orfèvre, c'est un extraordinaire niveau général de perfection." Otto Stoessl (*C. F. Meyer*, Die Literatur, Bd. 25 [Berlin, 1905], 58) finds "dass der Band der Meyerschen Gedichte vielleicht der einzige ist, welcher — ästhetisch genommen — kein schlechtes oder schwächeres Gedicht enthält."

148   1. Ge., 3.

2. Ge., 178; cf. Betsy Meyer, 15; Everth, 301; and the conclusion of the most recent treatment of Meyer which comes to hand, Frensdorf (34): "Am ungebrochensten er selbst aber ist er in seinen Gedichten, und am prägnantesten und klarsten scheint mir sein tiefstes Wesen in dem kurzen Gedicht 'Mövenflug' [*sic*] versinnbildlicht und zusammengefasst."

3. Maync, 389, 402.

149   1. Baumgarten, 210, 217, 219.

2. Everth, 22, 351; Faesi, 52. Cf. also E. Urbahn, "Symbolik in C. F. Meyers Gedichten," *Edda* 12, Bd. 23, H. 2 (1925), 161–274, and E. Hofacker, "Alte und neue Lyrik. C. F. Meyer und R. M. Rilke," *Monatshefte für Deutschunterricht*, XX, 8, 245–252.

3. Brw. Meyer-Rodenberg, 133.

150   1. Everth, 63, 351.

2. Baumgarten, 232; d'Harcourt, 214; Linden, 125, etc.

3. d'Harcourt, 214, 227–228.

4. Linden (125) feels, of course, "Jene Kräfte sind ihm der aesthetisch-konkrete und der ethisch-abstrakte Geist."

5. Br., I, 426–427, 429, to Carl Spitteler in answer to his specific question on this point. Cf. also Br., II, 381.

6. Cited by d'Harcourt, 278.

7. Br., I, 45.

151 1. Brw. Meyer-François, 93.
    2. Br., I, 128.
    3. d'Harcourt, 388, footnote 2. With Gallic quickness of perception this urbane French aristocrat discovers also in Schiller's sublime historical tragedies disturbing bourgeois and German middle-class elements. Cf. Robert d'Harcourt, *La Jeunesse de Schiller* (Paris [Plan], 1928), and my review of the same in *The Germanic Review*, V, No. 1 (January, 1930), 83–86.

152 1. Everth, 250. Cf. Gritta Baerlocher. *Die Geschichtsauffassung C. F. Meyers* (Heidelberg, 1922).
    2. Faesi, 80.

153 1. Brw. Meyer-François, 37.
    2. Everth, 347.
    3. "Genosse einer Schweizerfirma 'Keller und Meyer.'" (Bächthold, *Keller*, III, 286.) "Es ist nicht jedermanns Sache, ein siamesischer Zwilling zu sein." (Keller, *Sinngedicht*, cited by Wüst, 14.) For such a recent conventional comparison, cf. F. L. Pfeiffer, "Gottfried Keller and Conrad Ferdinand Meyer. A Comparison," *The Germanic Review*, II, No. 4 (October, 1927), 312–319.
    4. E. Schmidt, *Characteristiken*, I, 118; cf. Maync, *Vorrede*, X.

154 1. Cf. Oskar Walzel, *Vom Geistesleben alter und neuer Zeit* (Leipzig, 1922), 114–141 "Zwei Möglichkeiten deutscher Form."
    2. This is apparent even today to anyone who inspects in Zürich the birthplace of Keller in the *Alt-stadt* and the aristocratic residences on either side of the lake of Zürich, preferred by Meyer. An essential difference in their style of life is revealed also in Meyer's reference to the "Wirtshausumgebung und Weinatmosphäre zu der [Keller] durch den Coelibat verdammt war" (Br., II, 193), and Betsy Meyer's description of her brother's reaction to such establishments: "Bei seiner Abneigung, öffentliche Lokale und Weinstuben zu besuchen . . . er behauptete, schon der Geruch des Wirtshauses schlage ihm unangenehm auf die Nerven." — Betsy Meyer, 11.

156 1. To Kögel, quoted by Wüst, 93.
    2. Br., II, 508.

157 1. Br., II, 164.

2. Most common among these is an ungerman negative, for example: "und die mir erlauben, das Ewige Menschliche künstlerischer zu behandeln, als die brutale Aktualität zeitgenössischer Stoffe mir *nicht* gestalten würde" (Brw. Meyer-François, 12). Louise von François calls attention to his use of the double negative (Brw., 112), and Meyer replies, "Die italienische (mehr noch als französische) doppelte Negation wendete ich sehr gewissenhaft als Localton an." — *Ibid.*, 119.

3. Br., I, 33. On November 23, 1882, he assures Louise von François: "Jetzt bin ich sehr deutsch, pour ne plus changer." — Brw. Meyer-François, 76.

4. Br., I, 290.

5. Betsy Meyer, 75.

6. Br., I, 140, letter of October 18, 1890, to Felix Bovet.

158 1. Originally appeared in *La Bibliothèque Universelle* (November, 1864), under the title "Un nouveau poète Suisse," reprinted in part by Frey, 177–178.

2. Originally appeared in the *Schweizer Grenzpost,* December 28, 1885, reprinted in part by Frey, 78–79; d'Harcourt, 470.

3. Betsy Meyer, 65–66.

4. Brw. Meyer-François, 42.

5. d'Harcourt, 115.

159 1. Linden, 154.

2. Lusser, 47.

3. These terms I have more clearly defined in a paper before the Germanic Section of the Modern Language Association of America at Washington, December 31, 1930, entitled "The German Sense of Form" (cf. *PMLA*, XLV [1930], Supplement, LXIII), and before the College Art Association at New York, April 2, 1931, in a paper entitled "Form in German and Italian Art" (cf. *Parnassus,* III, No. 4 [April, 1931], 21). Both articles will be expanded before their final appearance in print.

4. Cf. the conclusion of my articles, "An Introductory Course in the History of German Civilization," *The German Quarterly*, II, No. 4 (November, 1929), 122–136,

and "German Dramas, Classic and Romantic," *The German Quarterly*, IV, No. 4 (November, 1931), 141–163.

160 1. Cf. my articles on Thomas Mann: "Thomas Mann's Treatment of the Marked Man," *PMLA*, XLIII, No. 2 (June, 1928), 561–568; "Thomas Mann's Appraisal of the Poet," *PMLA*, XLVI, No. 3 (September, 1931), 880–916; also *PMLA*, XLIV, No. 1 (March, 1929), 310–313; *ibid.*, XLV, No. 2 (June, 1930), 615. Also my article "A Course in Contemporary German Literature," *The German Quarterly*, III, No. 4 (November, 1930), 117–138.

The subject is specifically treated in an essay by Robert Faesi, "C. F. Meyer und Thomas Mann," in *Gestalten und Wandlungen schweizerischer Dichtung. Zehn Essais* (Zurich-Leipzig-Wien [Amalthea], 1922); also in his *C. F. Meyer*, 104, 134, 141, etc.

BIBLIOGRAPHY

BIBLIOGRAPHY

EVEN though the *Meyer-Bibliographie* by K. E. Lusser, long ago announced by Meyer's publisher Haessel, has not yet appeared in print, it is unnecessary to assemble here a complete list of the fairly numerous critical works that concern themselves with Conrad Ferdinand Meyer. As most of the more important of these are enumerated elsewhere either in the works cited below or in readily accessible bibliographical lists compiled by various scholarly journals (Euphorion, 1914, 1922 Ergänzungshefte 11 and 12, Neuerscheinungen der Jahre 1912–18; Jahresbericht über die wissenschaftlichen Neuerscheinungen auf dem Gebiete der neueren deutschen Literatur, Bd. 1, Bibliographie 1921, Berlin und Leipzig, 1924; Jahresberichte des Literarischen Zentralblattes, Germanische Sprachen und Literaturen, 1924 ff., Leipzig, 1925; and Zeitschrift für Deutschkunde, 1931, Heft 5, pp. 321–368), I can restrict myself to the following brief comments on editions of Meyer's works and letters and to the enumeration of the more helpful general and specialized critical works which are frequently referred to in the text and cited in the notes merely by indicating the author's name and page. Other less important works or articles appearing in periodicals as well as helpful works on aesthetics dealing with general problems of style have been indicated in the appropriate place in the notes by author and title or by such abbreviations as will, it is hoped, be found self-explanatory.

I have already set forth elsewhere in print my estimate of the more recent critical commentaries on Meyer ("Conrad Ferdinand Meyer, 1825–1925," *JEGP.*, XXVII, No. 4

[October, 1928], 486–495). Similar estimates of recent works on Meyer are the following:

Corrodi, Hans. C. F. Meyers Bild im Spiegel literaturwissenschaftlicher Erkenntnis. Schweizerische Monatshefte für Politik und Kultur, Jg. 3, Heft 9 (1923), 442–453.

Unger, Rudolf. Über und um C. F. Meyer. Die Literatur, XXVI, Heft 6 (March, 1924), 321–324.

Pongs, Hermann. Der Kampf um die Auffassung C. F. Meyers. Ztft. f. Deutschkunde, Jg. 1927, Heft 4, 257–277.

EDITIONS OF MEYER'S WORKS AND LETTERS

As there is no definitive critical edition of C. F. Meyer's works, I have referred to the old Haessel edition in nine volumes, which was for long the only one and which may still be looked upon as the standard despite the appearance of other more recent editions published by the same firm. The following chronological list of Meyer's works gives the abbreviations which I have used to designate them in the notes and the edition and date of every Haessel volume to which the abbreviations refer.

1864   Zwanzig Balladen von einem Schweizer. (Z.B.)
1870   Romanzen und Bilder. (R.B.)
1871   Huttens letzte Tage. (Hu.) (59, 1913)
1872   Engelberg. (E.) (23, 1913)
1873   Das Amulett. (A.) (Nov. I, 72, 1914)
1874   Jürg Jenatsch. (J.J.) (127, 1914)
1877   Der Schuss von der Kanzel. (S.) (Nov. I, 72, 1914)
1879   Der Heilige. (H.) (70, 1913)
1881   Plautus im Nonnenkloster. (P.) (Nov. I, 72, 1914)
1882   Gedichte. (Ge.) (69, 1914)
1882   Gustav Adolfs Page. (G.) (Nov. I, 72, 1914)
1883   Das Leiden eines Knaben. (L.) (Nov. II, 66, 1913)
1884   Die Hochzeit des Mönchs. (M.) (Nov. II, 66, 1913)
1885   Die Richterin. (R.) (Nov. II, 66, 1913)
1887   Die Versuchung des Pescara. (V.) (49, 1914)
1891   Angela Borgia. (A.B.) (39, 1914)

Of the newer editions published by Haessel in Leipzig the so-called *Neue Dünndruck Ausgabe* in four volumes presents a text revised by Herbert Cysarz, Jonas Fränkel, and Friedrich Michael and a treatment of Meyer's life and work by Robert Faesi. The so-called *Neue Taschenausgabe* in eight or fourteen volumes offers introductions to the various works written by Otto Blaser, Gottfried Bohnenblust, Walther Brecht, Emil Ermatinger, Otto von Greyerz, Harry Maync, and Max Nussberger. Recently other publishers have printed Meyer's complete works with competent editors; e g., Bong, editor, W. Linden; Knaur, editor, R. Faesi; Müller, editor, G. Steiner; Reclam, editor, M. Rychner.

Facsimile reprints of the original editions of Meyer's first three poetical works, *Zwanzig Balladen*, *Romanzen und Bilder* and *Huttens letzte Tage*, have also been published by Haessel. The same firm has also printed Meyer's unfinished prose works and the most important collection of his letters: Frey, Adolf, C. F. Meyers unvollendete Prosadichtungen, Leipzig (Haessel), 1916, 2 vols.; Frey, Adolf, Briefe Conrad Ferdinand Meyers, nebst seinen Rezensionen und Aufsätzen, Leipzig (Haessel), 1908–09, 2 vols. (abbreviated in the notes as Br.). Cf. Bertram, Ernst, C. F. Meyers Briefe, Mitt. d. Lit. Gesell. Bonn, Jg. 7, Heft 3, pp. 63–78 (1912).

Other letters have appeared in different periodicals and in three further collections in book form: Bettelheim, Anton, Louise von François und C. F. Meyer, Berlin und Leipzig (Reimer), 1920[2]; Langmesser, August, C. F. Meyer und Julius Rodenberg, Ein Briefwechsel, Berlin (Paetel), 1918; and d'Harcourt, Robert, C. F. Meyer; La Crise de 1852–56, Lettres de C. F. Meyer et de son entourage, Paris (Alcan), 1913 (abbreviated in the notes as Brw. Meyer-François, Brw. Meyer-Rodenberg, d'Harcourt, Crise, respectively).

GENERAL WORKS

Baumgarten, Franz Ferdinand. Das Werk Conrad Ferdinand Meyers. Renaissance-Empfinden und Stilkunst. München (George Müller), 1920². Cf. Everth, Erich — Ztft. f. Aesthetik, Bd. 13, pp. 77–97 (1918).

Everth, Erich. Conrad Ferdinand Meyer. Dichtung und Persönlichkeit. Dresden (Sibyllen-Verlag), 1924. Cf. also Everth, Erich — C. F. Meyers epischer Sprachstil, Ztft. f. Aesthetik, Bd. 20, 2, pp. 129–140 (1926).

Faesi, Robert. Conrad Ferdinand Meyer. Die Schweiz im deutschen Geistesleben, 36. Bändchen. Leipzig (Haessel), 1925.

Frey, Adolf. Conrad Ferdinand Meyer. Sein Leben und seine Werke. Stuttgart und Berlin (Cotta), 1919³.

d'Harcourt, Robert. C. F. Meyer. Sa vie, son œuvre. (1825–98). Paris (Alcan), 1913. Cf. Wüst, Paul — C. F. Meyer in französischem Lichte, Mitt. d. Lit. Gesell. Bonn, Jg. 11, Heft 1, pp. 1–30 (1918).

Langmesser, August. C. F. Meyer. Sein Leben, seine Werke und sein Nachlass. Berlin (Wiegandt und Grieben), 1905³.

Linden, Walther. Conrad Ferdinand Meyer. Entwicklung und Gestalt. München (Beck), 1922.

Maync, Harry. Conrad Ferdinand Meyer und sein Werk. Frauenfeld (Huber), 1925. Cf. Unger, Rudolf, Göttingische gelehrte Anzeigen, Jg. 191, Nr. 5, pp. 241–250 (1929).

Meyer, Betsy. Conrad Ferdinand Meyer. In der Erinnerung seiner Schwester. Berlin (Gebrüder Paetel), 1903.

SPECIALIZED TREATISES

Brecht, Walther. C. F. Meyer und das Kunstwerk seiner Gedichtsammlung. Wien und Leipzig (Braumüller), 1918. Cf. Maync, H. Das Literarische Echo, Jg. XXI, pp. 889–890 (1919).

Corrodi, Hans. C. F. Meyer und sein Verhältnis zum Drama. Leipzig (Haessel), 1923.

Frensdorf, Max. Conrad Ferdinand Meyer. Sein Werk und Wesen. Eisenach (Kühner), 1930.

Kalischer, Erwin. C. F. Meyer in seinem Verhältnis zur italienischen Renaissance. Palaestra, 64. Berlin (Mayer & Müller), 1907.

Kögel, Fritz. Bei C. F. Meyer. Ein Gespräch. Die Rheinlande, Monatschrift für deutsche Kunst, Jg. 1, Oktoberheft, pp. 27–33 (1900).

Köhler, Walter. C. F. Meyer als religiöser Charakter. Jena (Diederichs), 1911.

Korrodi, Eduard. C. F. Meyer-Studien. Leipzig (Haessel), 1912.

Kraeger, Heinrich. C. F. Meyer. Quellen und Wandlungen seiner Gedichte. Palaestra, 16. Berlin (Mayer & Müller), 1901.

Lusser, Karl Emanuel. C. F. Meyer. Das Problem seiner Jugend unter besonderer Berücksichtigung der deutschen und romanischen Bildungseinflüsse. Leipzig (Haessel), 1926.

Moser, Heinrich. Wandlungen der Gedichte C. F. Meyers. Leipzig (Haessel), 1900.

Nussberger, Max. Conrad Ferdinand Meyer. Leben und Werke. Frauenfeld (Huber), 1919.

Schröder, A. Kritische Studien zu den Gedichten C. F. Meyers. Köln (Gehly), 1928.

Wüst, Paul. Gottfried Keller und C. F. Meyer in ihrem persönlichen und literarischen Verhältnis. Leipzig (Haessel), 1911.

Wüst, Paul. C. F. Meyer-Probleme. Germanisch-Romanische Monatsschrift, Jg. 5, Hefte 6, 8, 9, pp. 297–307, 426–442 (1913).